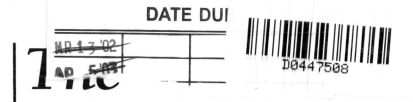
The

Articulate

Body

The
Physical
Training
of the Actor

Anne Dennis

DRAMA PUBLISHERS
an imprint of
Quite Specific Media Group Ltd.
New York

.N AND KATE

In memory of Etienne Decroux

For the sake of clarity "he" also means "she." And the reverse is also true. Perhaps the day will come when we can use "she" without causing it to jump off the page. We are all acutely aware of gender issues and anxiously await an unselfconscious resolution to the pronoun dilemma.
—The Publishers

Quite Specific Media Group Ltd.
260 Fifth Avenue
New York, NY 10001.

ISBN 0-89676-133-9

(212) 725-5377 v.   (212) 725-8506 f.
web: www.quitespecificmedia.com
email: info@quitespecificmedia.com

Quite Specific Media Group Ltd. imprints:
Costume & Fashion Press
Drama Publishers
By Design Press
Jade Rabbit
EntertainmentPro

Acknowledgments

THIS BOOK is very much the result of my students' enthusiasm, over a long period of time, for such a project. Without their inspiration, and indeed, insistence, the book would never have been written. Then too, there was the constant encouragement from Ognjenka Milicevic, Professor, University of Arts, Belgrade, whose belief in the need for such a book kept me going, when I could have easily slipped back into the rehearsal room or theatre space, rather than sitting at the computer. Many others have assisted the project by carefully reading the manuscript, by discussing the work at hand, by advising, by researching sources, etc. My thanks especially goes to J.N. Benedetti, Marian Malet, Ivan Jankovic, La Casona, Barcelona, Institut del Teatre, Barcelona, and Teatre de la Brume, Barcelona.

I wish to thank the following for helping to locate, identify and obtain permission to reproduce the photos: FilmoTeca del la Generalit de Catalunya; Kobal Collection, London; Institut Français de Barcelone; Goethe Institute, Barcelona; Jerry Pantzer, New York City; Editions du Seuil, Paris; Brecht-Archiv, Berlin; Berliner Ensemble, Berlin; The Adapters, New York City; Théâtre du mou-

vement, Paris; Els Joglars, Barcelona; La Casona, Barcelona; The-
atre de Complicite, London; Piccolo Teatro di Milano; Centre for
Performance Research, Cardiff; The Centre of Studies on Jerzy
Grotowski's Work and of the Cultural and Theatrical Research in
Wroclaw.

To my husband, Richard, my love and deep appreciation. His
constant patience, care and concrete help, throughout the process,
have made this book possible.

Contents

Introduction

The Actor is Perceived
and Theatre Begins

"To be on stage, you must have something to say."[1] This idea of Etienne Decroux, coupled with the vision of the actor who is able to present his thoughts with clarity and imagination, has remained fundamental and relevant to all my theatre work throughout the years. Thirty years ago, in the Eighth Avenue, New York City flat that served as Etienne Decroux's studio, I found such ideas to be the springboard for the study of the physically articulate actor. Here was the basis from which Decroux would realize his theatrical principles.

Since that time, my work has led me through many audiences, cultures, and influences, each one with a different demand on the theatre space and requiring a variety of theatre forms and skills. In these highly diverse situations, it has often been Decroux's words and thoughts, his sense of an actor's process that has offered a way forward. It is his perception of the actor as a communicator of ideas that has led me to insist that the actor's essential task is to present, clearly and effectively, the thoughts and feeling of the theatre event. It is this unique obligation to the audience that makes the actor the central element in the theatre space. In an art form often dominated by words, music, and visual effects, it is the actor who, rather than hiding behind these crutches, must develop, with confidence, this special relationship to the public. Theatre is a physical expression of interactions, relationships, and events. The actor, through visual images and sounds, is the catalyst.

It is necessary to break down the mystique that surrounds the "great actor," and begin to define that which makes the actor a good communicator. What is it that makes the public watch, listen, react? What resources must be available to the actor? To what purpose should an actor's craft be taught? How do the parts of the craft integrate to become the whole? Decroux dedicated most of his life to such a search. Certainly this book uses his work as the point of departure.

In order to establish a process that enables the actor to work with his maximum creative potential, it is necessary to define the physical elements specific to the actor's craft. How does the actor's physical task correspond to and differ from that of the dancer, the gymnast, or the circus performer? If it is through the body that the actor is able to articulate the objectives of the theatre piece, he must be provided with the knowledge of how concretely to make use of this instrument. Considerably more is involved than simply training an actor to be a "fit" person or a veritable virtuoso of performance skills. This book is not so much concerned with a "school" of training, but rather how the actor's craft is perceived: a concept of what an actor can be.

The actor informs through his "physicality."[2] Lights go up, the actor takes the space and is perceived by the audience, and theatre begins. A dramatic moment has been created and a response in the audience is imminent. Communication has begun. One can imagine theatre without words, or a set, or music. But, as Decroux was fond of reminding us, you cannot have theatre without the actor. In fact, it is exactly the actor's presence that defines theatre.

It follows to reason, therefore, that you cannot have articulate theatre without the skilled, articulate actor.

Etienne Decroux: a teacher of actors;
an actor's director.

PHOTO: JERRY PANTZER

PHOTO: JERRY PANTZER

PHOTO: JERRY PANTZER

Everything an actor does is seen and interpreted.
The Actor informs through his physicality: in silence
or voice; in motion or stillness.

Jean-Louis Barrault in "Hamlet".

Ernst Busch in "Life of Galileo."
COURTESY: BERLINER ENSEMBLE; PHOTO PERCY PAUKSCHTA

Helene Weigel in "The Mother."
COURTESY: BERLINER ENSEMBLE; PHOTO PERCY PAUKSCHTA

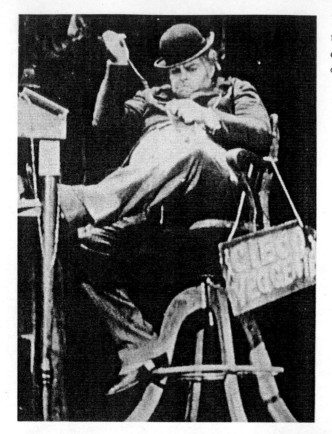

*T. Buazzelli as Peachum,
in "Threepenny Opera,"
directed by G. Strehler.*

*Rena Mirecka and
Ryszard Cieslak in
"The Constant Prince,"
Teatr Laboratorium.*

Mei Lan-fang, Chinese Drama actor of female ("Tan") roles.

The actor must find and present the essence of an interaction or relationship.

"*Encore Une Heure Si Courte.*"

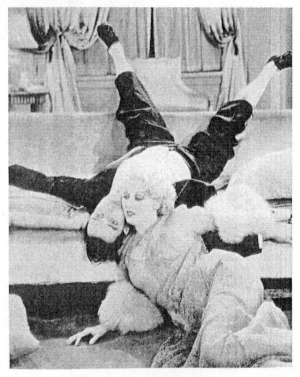

Buster Keaton in "Speak Easily."

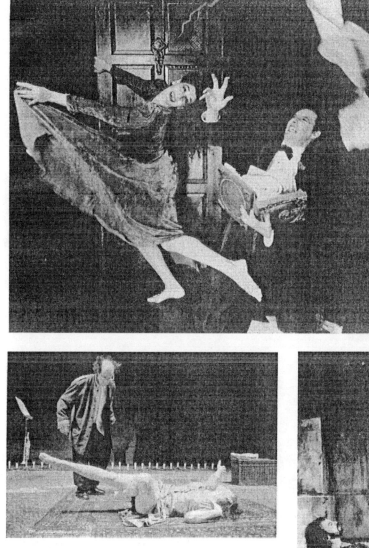

"Decodanz."

COURTESY: MARGOLIS/BROWN,
THE ADAPTERS COMPANY,
NEW YORK CITY;
PHOTO: RUBY LEVESQUE.

"El Nacional."

COURTESY: ELS JOGLARS, BARCELONA

"Antigona Kaiene."

COURTESY: LA CASONA, BARCELONA

Theatre is a collective art; actors create situations and images as well as characters.

"*The Visit.*"

"The Three Lives of Lucie Cabrol," based on a story by John Berger.

"*The Bed Experiment One.*"

1 | The Physically Articulate Actor

An actor's training must reflect the need for the physically articulate actor. Decroux often spoke of the acting exercises at Jacque Copeau's Ecole du Vieux Columbier in the Paris of the 1920s. Students, stripped of costumes, props, text, and set—their faces veiled, and their backs, as often as not, turned towards the audience—were required to make clear, dramatic statements. There must be no doubt in the audience's mind as to what the character is thinking or feeling; no uncertainty concerning where the character had come from and was going and precisely what each character wants. Everything about the character's social and psychological being must be made clear and visible. By working in this way, one could contemplate the specific physical skill that is unique to the actor—the need to master the physically explicit action.

It cannot be found in other movement techniques, nor is it a technique in itself. Rather it is a process through which the actor can achieve a vocabulary, a "grammar," a language that will provide the physical confidence necessary to perform with clarity no matter what the theatrical demand.

Everything the actor does is seen and interpreted. Physicality is central to the actor's expression: in silence or voice, in motion or stillness.

The actor's instrument, the body, must be well-tuned and able to reflect all the internal and external influences of the dramatic moment. There is simply no place for physical muttering or meandering; no room for haphazard movement, made in hopes that the audience will be able to second guess the meaning of the moment.

An actor is both "artist and instrument" (J.L. Barrault).[1] In the process of creating theatre, he will need a well-tuned, articulate instrument.

In theatre, ideas and feelings have value only if they are conveyed and understood. A thought or emotion must be explicit, no matter how small or subtle. The action—a parting, an embrace, a killing, etc.—gains its dramatic value through the moment that precedes it: a nagging moment of doubt or a moment of hesitation. To make sense of the whole, such moments must be visible.

Only with a clear understanding of what we mean by the "physically articulate actor" will we be able to train such an actor. If we are not simply talking about the actor who can somersault through space or who can perform a mean tap dance, then what do we mean? We know it when we see it. We remember the clear images left with us from productions by The Berliner Ensemble, or the companies of Dario Fo, Peter Brook, and Peter Stein. Moments in the work of Chaplin, Barrault, Marceau remain with us, etched in our minds. Recently I have seen remarkable physical clarity from the young actors of St. Petersburg and Moscow. They touch us and lead us to specific understandings of the dramatic event. They present us with images that make us think and want to know more. How is this achieved? How does the actor gain the ability to find and present the essence of a moment in a clear dramatic form?

Theatre demands from the actor a complete understanding and mastery of the possibilities of the acting craft. The actor must not remain trapped by his physical mannerisms and limitations. He must have an instrument that is physically responsive. He must be in control, ready to create.

Theatre is a reflection of its age and, in choosing what to present, comments upon it. It can act to influence, change, or preserve the social and historical moment. The actor, too, is a part of the cultural and political climate in which he finds himself. He is a product of his time, and the individual he has become will influence how he both approaches and presents his work. He must be up to this task. He must be free to explore and avoid imposing solutions. The work emerging will be his response to the historical moment. Nowhere is this more apparent than in the Europe of the 1990s, which finds peoples both merging together and simultaneously recoiling into the cultures and mores which have defined their past.

Documentary theatre, naturalistic theatre, ritualistic theatre, literary theatre, variety and cabaret—all reflect their historical moment. The actor must have the skills to make this happen.

The actor must be able to realize the demands of his imagination. He must have the physical acting skills necessary to create the characters and images that will make his objectives come to life (discussed further in Chapter Two), and he must have a strong, controlled, responsive instrument in order to achieve this goal (see Chapter Three). We are looking for an actor as articulate with his body as he is with words.

An Actor's work is concrete. It is precise and detailed. It demands that each part of the actor's instrument is tuned to respond to all internal and external influences; and these responses must be visible to the audience. The basis of the actor's craft is to reflect through his physicality all that is happening inside: to make the invisible visible.

2 | The Actor in the Performance Space

THE ACTOR DEFINES THEATRE. Without his presence, theatre does not exist. It is through the actor that an idea will be articulated. His means are image and sound. Often, however, the preparation of the actor's "means" of expression has been separated from the study of acting and the rehearsal process. Physical training has been seen as a classroom activity. The body is being prepared, but the question "for what" is not addressed. The young actor, as if by magic, is expected to take the straight, strong, coordinated, neutral body he has been nurturing, together with a smattering of skills from dance, tumbling and circus classes, and be able to create a clear character, making a clear visual statement.

It does not happen this way. The result is that the studious classroom actor often finds himself falling back into old habits the minute he is in the rehearsal space. Under the pressure of learning lines, of "delivering" lines, of being heard, of finding characters and objectives, it is all too easy to return to the safe "tricks" that have served him "well enough" in the past. The process of physicalizing the space and the people (characters) in the space is left to chance. It is hoped that these things will happen by themselves.

Some directors and companies, such as those of Peter Brook or Dario Fo, give a great deal of time and space to physical process. Other directors and companies, however, use warm-up "games" as an end in themselves. Questions concerning physical expression, as it relates to the performance, are ignored. The actor "trips about the stage, like a child in his/her mother's party dress" (Decroux), in search of a character that will be visible to the audience. Externals begin to be added—a hump here or a limp there, a frilly hat or a dramatic cape. However, there is no body underneath to carry these crutches, and all visual clarity collapses the moment the actor moves or speaks. The physical character is not present, and the actor, once again, must rely on charisma to be interesting and to hold the audience visually.

This chapter is concerned with these questions and attempts to find a process to help the actor along. Movement must never be seen as a separate skill, something which can be added on as an afterthought. It must be seen to be a part of the acting craft, well integrated into the task of acting.

The Body: The Source of an Actor's Expression

Having a well-tuned instrument is not enough. The actor must know how to use his instrument with imagination and skill. Actors, in collaboration with other theatre workers (the designers, technicians, directors, and writers), are searching for theatrical clarity, through which they can convey their ideas.

In order to communicate clearly, actors must be clear themselves. They must be able to analyze and research their material and come to clear decisions. Once excited by and opened to the material, they will find that one idea leads to another. They must then search, discover, discard, and rework their ideas and, along with the rest of the company, bring them alive in the theatre space through theatrical language. Only if an actor is clear himself, will he be able to respond physically to the dramatic situation being created. In early days of rehearsal, the exact manner in which a performance is to develop will necessarily be vague. But there is no place for vagueness in the actor's process. Directions such as "use the space" are useless. The first thing an actor should be very clear about is his physical action: Who is he in the space and what does he want?

However, taking an action or doing something believable in the theatre space does not, in itself, make theatre. An action must be seen to be an expression of human behavior—coming from somewhere, and going somewhere. Movement for the actor is not, in itself, an "instrument to express," though it could be said to be so in some forms of dance. Rather, it is the result of and response to a "need" (a motivation) to move. The body is simply the instrument that reflects that need.

Actions such as falling on one's face or even digging up a dead body are meaningless in themselves. The audience must know who is doing the action, and in what social and psychological context. If the Pope falls on his face, it is substantially a different matter from the football hooligan, with a lot of lager under his belt, falling on his face! The action may be the same but will have a very different dramatic value.

At all costs the actor must avoid generalized actions and motions (gestures) if he is to arrive at the essential. The physically clear actor is not replacing words with gesture, e.g., the wiping of a brow to say "I am hot" or the holding of the back and quivering of the hand to say "I am old. He is, rather, struggling to find the physical essence of the situation. This is how I understand Bertolt Brecht's use of the term "gestus" when speaking of the actor's physical attitude and actions. It is important to think not in terms of illustrating an idea but rather physicalizing the contradictions and conflicts that constitute the dramatic moment. We are after clarity without explanation. Words must come out of the physical need to communicate and offer a further language. As the audience watches, there must be no doubt in its mind as to what the character is doing, thinking, and feeling.

Finding the essential involves selection. What we keep and what we discard—our decisions and choices—these are the questions of an actor's creativity.

Internal and external influences will cause (motivate) the physical response. The reaction may be one of stillness, or the mere flicker of an eyelid. The character moves only because he must. Who he is, where he is, what the surrounding circumstances are, will all affect just how the movement manifests itself.

List Pisk, in her very personal book, has said that "... the shape of your body is the outer boundary of inner contents."[1] In order to achieve this, the actor's character must be well defined both in thought and physicality. Otherwise he will rely on generalities and simply not be credible.

We often see the actor crossing the stage and perhaps sitting down only because the director has told him to do so. The director, with the scene's overall objective in mind, may himself be clear when he gives this direction. But there may be, as well, no readily apparent reason for the character not just to remain where he is. The actor may feel blocked, unable to motivate the action, and the cross becomes an inconsequential excess. The actor has not made the decisions necessary to motivate the move. He is therefore without the basis to build the dramatic moment. The movements will seem empty, unbelievable. That same actor would probably never speak a line unless it was an integrated part of the moment. But he will move, lacking the same clarity he has demanded from himself in relationship to the text. "Line readings"—Never! Decorative movements—one sees them so often!

To gain the physicality of a character the actor must follow all the rules of the acting craft. A character develops and emerges from the actor's neutral body. The body is neutral, but the actor inside is not. His creative imagination will be responding to the stimuli of the previous work—the research and the decisions he has made. As the actor begins to work physically, the information and physical feelings begin to merge, and the character's neutral body begins to take form. What it must not be is merely an imitation of some other physicality, heaped onto the actor's body. All bodies are the result of a specific history, of specific circumstances. This requires a specific physical process that must be allowed to happen. Once developed, the sustaining of a character's physicality in the artificial demands of the theatre space is a matter of concentration and technique. Actors have a tendency to be clear as long as they are engaged in the action vocally and then "to die" on the stage as soon as they are still or silent. To avoid this, the character's inner monologue must be as precise as his spoken lines. The source of his thoughts is as important as the source of his spoken words.

An actor is often surprised by just how unclear he has been. He has thought himself "truthful," only to find the audience has remained confused throughout. Clarity depends on precise objectives, clearly manifested through action.

If conflict is the source of drama, the actor must learn to enjoy these conflicts with a physical élan and freedom. With flair, he must develop such moments and not merely sweep them under the carpet. The actor must learn to confront without negativity. Confrontation is a good concept for the actor—a key to action. "I will confront him." The moment can then open up.

Perhaps one of the greatest causes of confusion in the young actor is the need to "go for" and maintain his objectives and yet retain, to a certain extent, an awareness through his "third eye" of himself as the audience sees him. Certainly he must "listen" to those watching—to be able to play not just for but with the audience. He must be aware of tentative moments and be able to develop them. He must pay attention to detail and yet discard all excess. He must find the scene's focus. In this, directors and others watching outside the action can be immensely helpful.

An actor's work on physicality will begin in the same manner, whether he is performing in a "naturalistic" play or a piece of "physical theatre." The well-trained actor will have the craft to move from style to style, governed by his concern over the best way possible to present an idea and the artistic decisions that follow. Theatre must not be limited by the actor's lack of skill.

The Character's Body Takes Over the Actor's Body

A character's body is a concrete, visible entity, and not an abstract, philosophical idea. Therefore it must not be created solely in abstraction from the imagination of the actor. It must be the result of careful analysis that will provide the actor's imagination with a point of departure, a point from which to take off and fly. The actor must be aware of all the influences that have formed his character. It is this melange of personal and cultural history which will provide the basis for a character's physicality. It is the basis for his emotional and intellectual responses as well. *The actor must go beyond appearances and imitation.*

The actor must plunge into the work in a physical manner, identifying, reproducing and sustaining a physicality *that has resulted from analysis and imagination.* A body is not developed through intellectual decisions.

There are many ways to take this plunge. Peter Brook, in *The Shifting Point"*[2] speaks of a "mixture of means": improvising, analysis, etc.. Anything goes, as long as it is under control and the direction is clear. The actor must be both sensitive and concrete as he delves into the influences on a character's life. Most important, the actor must be open, and yet aware. Finding his character will make him vulnerable and require a willingness to take risks. When the actor takes the easy way out, opting for generality and imitation, he finds that he is physically bound and gagged. He has severed himself from the basis from which the character could grow and develop.

The actor must not slip into decisions made outside the process; e.g., how the character will sit down or walk, etc. The actor must first find the body and only then sit down with it. If the physicality is clear, then the body will respond in accordance to the situation.

An open actor will not avoid contradictions but revel in them. They are the meat of theatre. Take, for example, the frail old lady who, from her armchair, runs the household with an iron grip. Think about the huge, strong man who is simply terrified at the thought of receiving an injection.

Over and over again Decroux would say, "Do not play pathos."

What he meant was, do not generalize emotion. Don't play "love," "pain," "sadness," "in-love" etc; rather listen, react, respond.

The physical reaction is totally dependent on the character, who he is and what he wants. Different characters, for example, will react differently to "being-in-love." It is not a state in itself. One character may feel "as light as a feather," ready to fly. Yet another may find himself "oppressed" by such love, weighted down as if he were carrying rocks on his shoulders. When, for instance, a character says, "I love you," does he want to be swept off his feet, or rather does he want a brief kiss on the forehead and be allowed to turn over and go to sleep?

The Actor Must Gain Control: Identifying the "Physical Feeling"

A strong man walks far, for a specific reason, and becomes exhausted. His body will *feel* different from that of a weak man walking the same distance for the same reason. This *feeling* is what I call the "physical feeling." It is the actor's task to be able to create this feeling, to identify it, to analyze it, and then to sustain it throughout the changing demands of the theatre piece. Finally, he must be able to recreate this concrete feeling, performance after performance. The actor must be able to rely on his understanding of the physical neutrality of the character and be open to the character's physical development. In order for an actor's impulse to be free to declare itself, it must be unblocked and uncluttered by the actor's body. Otherwise, the impulse will become lost, confused, or simply remain stifled.

The actor must be able to sustain the physical feeling (the body, the mood) at all times; even if he finds himself flying through the air! It is exactly at such moments that the actor, working through imitation, will tend to lose or "drop" his character. As a result, he will drop his motivation for the movement, as well, and he will return to his own physicality. He will grope for a way to get back that which he has externally created and has now lost. It doesn't necessarily take flying through space for this to happen to an actor. Often, sitting down on a chair is enough!

· We are looking for the physically responsive actor. We have said that this implies considerably more than a fit actor with a few extra skills in his pocket. However, methods to achieve this goal are not always included in the process of an actor's physical training. Integrating physicality into theatre expression requires a process. When something happens in the theatre space, theatre begins. Drama emerges. The space, even a completely still space, becomes alive. Interactions or a lack of interactions (which is an interaction of sorts!) provide the stimuli—internal or external—to which the actor can react. The creative impulse is dependent on finding this stimulus. The impulse, the actor's reaction to the stimulus, must then be physically expressed in order to be understood. It is not good enough just to be "felt" by the actor.

How the character moves must not be based on the actor's body, but rather on the character's body in the specifically given circumstances. A character's physicality is not merely a question of a walk or how the arms are dangled. It is not enough to give the character a limp or other physical change. The actor must recreate the physical feeling of his character's specific limp, which is the result of a specific body under specific social and emotional circumstances.

This physical feeling must be *detailed*, e.g., how does the back react to the limp when sitting or walking? It must be *developed*, e.g., what is specific about this particular limp? It is, after all, the result of a specific history, of a specific body, and cannot be generalized. It must be *integrated*, e.g., how does this man with a limp behave? How does his social and emotional being respond to the influences about him? The actor must not preconceive these responses, but rather allow his physical being to be his source of discovery. To become credible, the actor must find, through his own body, the physical experiences of the character.

Physically clear acting requires a keen visual imagination. The actor must be free to open up to the situation. Only with a well-defined physicality is this possible. Impulses must be taken to their physical conclusion. Imagination and a sense of risk must take the character forward.

An actor's freedom therefore implies the gaining of control of the dramatic moment. In fact, the actor must be able to take on such a moment and find new ways to clarify and enhance his response. He must be able to find ways to take the moment to new depths. There must always be space and freedom to grow. The actor must never be a slave to external or imposed patterns or generalities.

Theatre is an ensemble art. The actor is a part of the whole, responding within the rhythm, design, intensity, and focus of the theatre image. Through offering and receiving, discarding and developing, the actor will find the visual essence of an idea or moment.

"EVERYTHING MUST BEGIN FROM THE INTERIOR—IF OUTWARD, ONLY FORM" (DECROUX)

Who a character is will determine how he gets what he wants (his intentions). The social and psychological specifics of the character as well as the specifics of the space and circumstances will influence the action. An actor's gesture or movement is nothing other than a physical response to his motivation. It begins in the inside and comes out with the breath. An actor must never move for a movement's sake, e.g., to look good. The character moves as a result of his intentions, in order to achieve what he wants. A step or walk is meaningless if it does not reflect the character's need to move. A state of being cannot be presupposed. Rather it emerges, depending on what has gone before, what is happening now, and what may happen in the future. The actor enters this moment, his physicality having been defined from the past. He is, at the moment he enters, the result of all he has been and done. New influences will react with the old physical feelings—the moment can take off.

To presuppose, to demonstrate, to pretend, to anticipate, and to generalize are unnecessary. For the actor who has found his physicality, based on physical feeling (the muscularity, the breath, the tensions, the outside and inside influences), there is simply no need for these crutches. They will only hinder. The physically astute actor will not need to give us a mish-mash of externalized images and feelings. He must work with a faith in the intelligence of the audience to interpret that which he is clearly stating.

The actor's task is to create and project. Barrault reminds us that theatre is not "just a place for personal exhibitionism."[3] I would add to this the word "virtuosity." Even less is it a place for charisma. An actor has a responsibility to the idea of the piece and to the audience who is in the position of receiving. His work is not that of manipulating or imposing. That is exhibitionism. Rather he must stimulate the audience to think and to respond with intellect and feeling. And he must be in control of his craft in order to do this.

An actor's physical training, therefore, goes beyond physical performance skills. It must, first of all, be concerned with an actor's immediate needs to be clear and credible for the audience. Theatre deals with artificial space, and, as a result, the actor cannot merely represent or repeat reality. An actor, for example, must fall without injuring himself. But knowing how to fall is not enough. The fall must be in character and in response to a specific dramatic moment. It is the reason, or cause of the fall that will dictate the specific manner in which the character will fall. An actor must have the technique that will, in turn, free him to execute the dramatic demands of the moment. One must not negate physical skills, but rather understand their use.

The actor's process of character development must begin with the detailed, ordinary, naturalistic reality of who his character is, and how he got to be who he is. It is this process that will provide the actor with the basis from which he may be able to continue to analyze, and, along with the theatre collective, search for the best way to make a theatrical statement. By its very structure, theatre is not and cannot be an objective mirror image of real life. Time, focus, and selection are the devices with which theatre workers will prepare their work. Their struggle is to find the best means possible to guide the audience. Brecht called theatre "heightened" naturalism.[4] I believe that this explains what the search is about. In other words, we choose what to emphasize, what to discard. Decroux spoke of taking "the ordinary into the extraordinary in order to see the ordinary more clearly." The famous Russian clown Popov spoke of combining "organically, eccentricity with realism."[5]

The Actor's Tools: Analysis
with Imagination

THE ANALYSIS OF THE TEXT AND MATERIAL

The actor must begin with great diligence to collect and understand detail. One must never be lazy about detail. In the end, it will define the essence of the character.

As the content of the text or piece is analyzed, decisions have to be made concerning the primary objectives: What does the play want and what do the characters want? Through discussions and improvisations, impressions will take form and decisions will be made; the skeleton of the character will gradually emerge, come off the page, and into the performance space. In the process, more and more is learned. The greater the number of details at an actor's disposal, the easier it is for him to put flesh on this skeleton. He looks for hints in the text. He looks at what other characters say about or do with his character. He goes through the text, line by line, bringing every action verbally alive, by describing it vividly, using adverbs such as reluctantly, warmly, suspiciously, etc. Finally, he looks at *how* the character acts and reacts. "A body must not mime a text; but move inside and with it." (Decroux) .[6] After analysis of the text, one begins to take a long, hard look at the character and at the influences on it.

AN AUTOBIOGRAPHY IS ESTABLISHED

In creating the life of a character, the actor's imagination will now come to the forefront. He will need to take into consideration all that he has learned in the previous step. The character's history, both cultural and personal, will be the starting point from which the character's life will emerge. All details, i.e., age, work, climate, status, class, and the like will mingle to form the physicality and psychology of this character.

The actor must look in great detail at all the influences in a character's life. The cultural influences, such as national history, work, class, and status affect and, in turn, are affected by personal physical and emotional reactions to age, health, environment, climate, familiarity, and physical comfort. *An actor will need to go beyond his own experience to understand a character*. He must make concrete and visible that which is alien to him. Notice how this differs in the following examples:

A character may feel "uplifted" with pleasure. The word, in itself, is meaningless for the actor. How this feeling will be manifested is what is interesting, and in this context the word might even prove helpful in providing an actor with yet another clue. But all reactions will vary, depending on the many possible, differing influences present in the dramatic moment. Like an alchemist, the actor must put his clues together and perhaps come up with a substance quite new to him. An actor cannot limit himself to his own personal circumstances and experiences. He must never tire of investigating all the possibilities surrounding him.

A character in a play feels "embarrassed" and would like to disappear. A world leader, closely followed by the media, will necessarily react in a manner quite different from that of a small child, who with similar feelings, may just crawl under the table.

The "smile" of the character may represent different things in different cultures. It is not representational of a universal feeling. In the USA, it has been traditional to smile for a photo ("say cheese"). This may well be a very different smile from the eastern smile of politeness or the adolescent smile of embarrassment.

A seemingly universal emotional reaction, such as retreat in the face of fear, will be greatly influenced by specific social implications that may severely affect actions and reactions. Will a character turn and flee or will the retreat merely be reflected in the furtive glances?

How *do* social structures influence peoples' physicality? For a start, think of an Italian and a Dane in the same dramatic situation. A character's age, self-image, and health are important factors as well.

The influence of work (what one has done with one's body over a period of time, in specifically defined social circumstances) is one of the most interesting studies for the actor. Not only is the actual physical activity itself in question, but one must also look at the emotional and social attitude towards that particular work from an historical perspective. How the character perceives his work and what status it brings him, will greatly affect the physicality of the character.

Dress and costume deserve a special note because, though no one denies their great influence on a character's physicality, I have experienced a loathing on the part of actors to get out of their trainers and tracksuits, especially in early days of rehearsal. To understand and achieve the physical feeling of a character, the actor must rehearse in costume, ersatz though it may be. Corsets, pointed shoes, high heels—all will cause the character to feel and move in specific ways. Often it is the social image of the clothes, or the mud at the hem of a skirt, or the tightness of a belt or the pinch of the shoes that will absolutely dictate the physical feeling of the moment. Imagine a long skirt, mud dripping from the hem, sweeping into an elegant drawing room. Imagine a knee-length skirt, worn by an elderly lady who, when sitting on the bus, can no longer manage to keep her knees together. There are hundreds of such examples. The character's physical reactions to such moments are what makes him three dimensional and vital to the audience. The use of such externals, such as the essential costume or prop, all help to guide the actor to his inner resources.

The autobiography will bring clarity to the actor and therefore to the audience. Its purpose is to make the character alive and believable. The actor must reject all temptations to embellish and decorate the character and by doing so take it beyond the realms of credibility.

A DAY IN THE LIFE OF THE CHARACTER

After establishing the autobiography of the character, the actor must contemplate a day in his life. This involves a moment by moment, detailed analysis of the character' day. The actor must look at how a typical day would evolve and how the character responds to its' differing demands. What does the character do when he wakes in the morning? How does he behave in the bathroom or in front of a mirror? How does he go to work? What does he physically do when he eats, argues, makes love? What are his night habits? *A clear, detailed description of his behavior will provide real clues for the actor.* It will also provide the actor with the basis for much physical "business" and activity that he may want to develop.

RELATIONSHIP AND PERSONAL HISTORY
WITH OTHER CHARACTERS

Actors do not develop their roles in isolation. Together, the ensemble of actors, directors, and others must discuss, in detail, all they have discovered through improvisation and play analysis. The more they find, the more they will be able to explore and develop through the practical exercises. If certain feelings are sensed, such as "hesitation" or "straightforwardness", they can be taken further and allowed to filter organically into the work. Interactions grow and new aspects of the relationships will be constantly discovered or rather uncovered. Listening to one another, with great physical sensitivity, is the basis of the work. Actors must not simply be open; they must also be generous.

ANALYSIS OF THE DRAMATIC MOMENT

In order for a dramatic moment to happen, the actors must understand the objective of the moment as well as who they are in the space and what they are doing there. Questions must be asked. Answers must be found.

Where did you come from?
Where are you going?
What do you want?
How will you get it?

As these questions are answered, that which I refer to as the "dramatic moment" will form. However, these answers must not be the result of an intellectual decision, but rather emerge from play, through interaction—*through action*. Everything a character does waits, sits, sleeps, plays, dresses, smokes, and the like, is the result of his emotional and physical makeup in the face of situations and circumstances. *There is no room for generalities and clichés.*

In order to achieve these moments, the actor will be concerned with what is commonly referred to as the "physical actions" of his character. He must always remember that it is *the situation that is moving and thought provoking.* "The event is what is interesting," said Decroux. One must not play emotion, but rather find what a character does, in a specific situation. The actor must listen, receive, react to all that is happening. I understand voice and sound to be a physical response, as well as movement. How the actor reacts—what he does—will be based on all he has learned about his character. With his character's "physical feelings" clearly established, he will have the possibility for an impulse to emerge as action. In my opinion, if the actor does not know his character well, in a social and historical context, it will be impossible to make clear decisions and impossible to find or define physical actions. Decisions must be flexible, ready to be changed if they are not providing the basis for clear action. But one cannot begin without clarity. *Actions come out of a character.* The character's body and physicality will therefore help define the action or "beat." *What* one wants, and *how* one gets it will depend on *who* is doing the action. It is not enough to think "colorfully." One must think in character. How and what one does depends on who one is, physically. This physicality is affected by internal and external influences. They, in turn, will influence how the character responds to his own emotional (internal) and social (external) situations. Actors must first work with physicality. They must identify "physical feelings" and not be lead by lines or text.

Physical Feelings: Creating the Illusion of a Character's Physical Being

By analyzing the physical process of what actually happens to a body under specific conditions, actors can understand, recreate, and therefore physically feel specific sensations that would ordinarily be beyond their own personal physical experiences. In reproducing, through breath, through muscles, and through tension levels what occurs physically to a body when touched by external (eg.,weather) or internal (e.g.,emotional) influences, the actor can begin concretely to identify how a body, other than his own, actually "feels." By placing the weight, by finding where the breath is centred, by finding to what extent the muscles are taut, or elastic or flabby, the actor will have a process through which he can "clock" a physical feeling and at any time be able to recreate, apply, and develop it, as needed. It is simply a method to increase the actor's physical vocabulary. He can begin to understand what he has felt and what other bodies feel—the causes and effects of physicality. Through an understanding of how both external and internal influences affect the body—the muscular, skeletal, nervous, and respiratory structures—the actor can reproduce the physical feelings in his character's body. A body and its physical state can thus, organically, emerge. The actor is pro- vided with a concrete basis to rebuild, to recreate, night after night, a believable physicality.

If, for example, a character has lost his muscular elasticity through age, he will need to breathe in a shallow manner, that, in turn, will necessitate a specific manner of holding himself and moving. Or if a character cannot depend on the muscles of his legs and feet to hold him up, he may well find that such a weakness will cause a fear of falling and the need to have a stick or hold on to a wall or another person. *The action, however, must be the result of a physical feeling that causes the emotional feeling, which will result in a physical response to the emotion.* The actor must identify the motor (cause) of an action.

A body must be free to act and interact. Only if the physicality has become his own, integrated into the body of the actor, can this happen without constant reassessment and rearrangement. If the actor pretends to have a hump on his back, he will need to constantly remind himself of the fact, and to readjust everything to that physical state. If, however, the actor can create in his body the physical phenomenon of how it feels to have a specific hump (the muscular and skeletal realities of the particular condition), he will have a concrete feeling that will influence all his other movements and activities. This physical feeling remains and develops, as new sources influence it (e.g., age, climate, health). The body will follow the character into new situations. If the actor begins to lose the feeling, he has a concrete method to refind, to rebuild it again.

In Epic Theatre, a character may often be required to leave his body, comment on actions, and then reenter where he left off. Not an easy task. But recreating a physical feeling is a concrete activity that provides the actor with a way back into the character he has just left. Simply placing a body back into a predetermined position is external, abstract, and hard to "get right." The actor has no basis from which to begin, other than a picture in his head.

Finding the "physical feeling" is a process with which the actor can build the physical manifestation of a body in a dramatic moment. In this way he is able to assimilate physically all the known facts and details and then, using his imagination, fill in the gaps. The first step is to identify the feeling and then work to recreate what has been found, until it becomes one's own.

How do we approach this process? What are the questions we need to pose? I would suggest we start with: "What actually happens to the body when..." When one is hot or cold? When one is blind? When one has tuberculosis? The actor must avoid "showing" the audience that the character has tuberculosis by coughing. He must find the physical feeling that causes the cough and then allow the cough to happen or perhaps try to suppress it, depending on the actor's decision in the context of the dramatic moment. The clue to this work is often found in the breath (how certain physical conditions affect breathing) and in the tension to be found in isolated muscles (under which specific conditions will certain muscles contract). The actor must be well aware that this is a method to find a reality and be ready to adapt this reality to the demands of the theatre space. The actor will still need to breathe in such a way that he can continue to speak and to "act." The actor must always be conscious of the illusion involved. He will need to modify his physical "truth," if he is to control the theatre space. But, he must begin by reproducing the physical feeling as closely as possible and then make use of it to create something believable and sustainable. For example, getting a physical understanding of what blindness is and how it "feels" may be achieved by concocting a situation where the actor cannot see, or expect to see. (What is the difference, for example of a blind man walking in the pitch dark or a sighted man in the same situation?) In the performing space the feeling of sightlessness can be achieved by wearing contact lenses. This will give the actor a "feeling" to identify, on which he can base his work. He may decide to continue to work with the lenses but, if not, he will have a concrete "feeling " and understanding, which he can now recreate and which will provide a basis for his work.

One cannot be credible as a specific drunk person simply by playing drunk or imitating a drunk person one has watched. One must analyze what exactly is happening to this specific, inebriated body. The actor must not try to reproduce his own drunk experience, but rather, understand physically, the character and his situation. An unsteady walk is not enough. In fact, what is the difference between the unsteady wobble of the drunk and of the toddler? To find the answer the actor must find the effect of alcohol on muscles, on focus, on balance, on concentration. He can thus recreate these feelings into the previously defined physicality of his character. This, in turn, will dictate what actually happens to his character the moment he tries to put one foot in front of the other, or gets up from a table and realizes that he had better not try to move. He will perhaps identify the sour taste of red wine in his mouth at the moment he is about to receive a kiss! The actor, creating the toddler, would need to ask very similar questions, and would get very different answers. In either case, it is not simply a question of stumbling about or falling over. This method will permit the actor to find the unfamiliar. He will be able to find a feeling he has never felt before: extreme heat, old age, pregnancy, drunkenness, or other condition.

We are looking for a methodology that will help the actor go beyond his personal experience and yet reproduce a physicality more dependable than through mere imitation. We are looking for a methodology which will allow the actor to take that which he knows (his own experiences), along with that which he has analyzed, and then, through these understandings, identify feelings he does not know from direct experience. He is making the *unfamiliar tangible*. The actor will no longer be limited to his own life experiences or bound to all the pitfalls of imitation.

Never been cold? Then what is it to shiver? Never been middle-aged? Then what happens to the body as it gets older? Language often aids in discovering the unfamiliar. Try to identify what certain words imply. We often say that someone is as cold "as a fish" or "wobbly as jelly" or that his hands are "clammy." We speak of heat as "oppressive," or sometimes it is "boiling hot" and we feel as if we are "melting." We say that old age causes one to be "brittle" and "fragile." When cold, one can be "frozen stiff"; the cold itself is "biting." People seem to "burst" or "explode" or feel "high" when full of energy.

There is simply *no need for imitation*. The actor must find and analyze, layer by layer, the physicality of his character. A character is credible when the physical action comes from within the character and is not simply applied onto the character's form.

In order to find the walk of a character, the actor must understand that the walk is not imposed on a body, but rather, the result of it. Placing the body in a specific position we have seen or imagined, will not accomplish a credible walk. *A movement must evolve and become a whole.* The walk is only a manifestation of the whole, as indeed, is all other physicality.

A body's movement is the result of the physical and emotional being who happens to be moving in specific circumstances. When we first see someone from a distance coming down the street, what is it about the image we see that immediately allows us to identify the person and know it can be no one else? What is the essence of that far off silhouette that tells us so much?

With a firm grasp of the character's body, the actor will be able to understand and "feel" his character as he becomes "exhausted," or in a "terrible rush," or even "smitten."

Gesture must come from the character and not from "someone I know, a bit like him." How many old people really hold their backs or mumble or even have sticks? Do all children, of all ages, really pick their noses and eat snot? It's too easy! Generalities, such as these, present to the audience two-dimensional characters who will be, necessarily, limited; they have come from no where and have no way to develop organically. *We are looking for an external physicality dictated to by an internal source,* and reflecting the very essence of a character—his thoughts and his feelings. We are *making the invisible, visible.*

We always expect the eyes to reflect what is inside a person. But the arm, the knee, the feet, the back—these, too, can be a reflection of the inner person. Unfortunately, despite both enormous will and energy, many actors are so physically limited as to be able to reveal only from the neck up. (In Spain, I have heard it said that actors act from the waist up!)

Physicality isn't a question of form, but rather how the internal is reflected through the body. The situation and the character's objectives will dictate how this character physically responds and manifests himself. Breath is the key. It reflects emotion and is expressed through the chest. Think about how grief or happiness affect breathing. Through breath, feelings become visible. "Breath is the best interpreter of emotion, as look is for thought." (Decroux). It permits the psychology of the moment to be expressed in concrete terms. The audience will be aware of the emotion, by way of the breath and the action it causes. Decroux also noted that "anxiety leads to petrifaction." A good thought for the actor. Without relaxation and breath, he will be blocked and can't work.

INTENTION CAUSES THE ACTOR TO MOVE IN RESPONSE

Movement and sound in the theatre space are the physical manifestation of a character and/or interaction in the dramatic moment. Movement and gesture are not separate entities, happening apart from the whole. If a gesture is not right for that moment, there is something wrong with the process and the actor must go back and rebuild. The job of the actor, the director, and the movement director is to analyze the movement in relation to the character within the given moment.

If the source is wrong, find another! That is what I mean by "an actor's imagination." Similar ideas have been expressed by other theatre people: Decroux, List Pisk, and R.G.Davis in his article "Method in Mime."[7] We are all referring to a way of working that simply allows for the *motivating external movement from internal sources*.

FINDING THE ESSENCE OF THE DRAMATIC MOMENT

It is through detail that the actor will discover the basis from which he can discard all excess. Clarity concerning the detail will permit the actor to discard with intelligence and sensitivity. The actor, in control, has choice. Each movement, no matter how small—the tilt of the head or flick of the wrist—is seen, and carries with it a dramatic value. When and how much focus to bring to a movement is a question of creativity. Ultimate clarity comes from minimum movement. Even chaos and clutter have their essence.

One cannot get to the essence, without having done the work—without having found the details and made the decisions. "Avoid through-lines and get to the details," drama teacher and director

Karl Weber used to lecture his actors while directing a Brecht play! An actor, armed with detail, has the means to avoid clichés and generalities. First the actor must find and define. Then he can begin to eliminate all that is peripheral, stripping down the quotidian and putting a life into three hours (or as a poet or mime will often do, into three minutes).

The "gestus" and physical attitudes that remain must provide clear physical statements. They are not representations or illustrations of words or phrases. "Gesture" is a dangerous word because it often implies a movement that explains. What we are talking about is a total physical attitude that like a poem, captures a moment. The actor is looking for the clearest "gestus," the physical presence and action (or reaction) that will allow the audience to be clear about the objective of the dramatic moment. This "gestus" must not be imposed. It comes from somewhere and must be the response to something. The actor must find this moment through a dramatic process, just as he did his physical actions.

What the gestus is not : "Oh!" the actor exclaims, "I understand. My character is pleading. Now, let me find an appropriate pleading gesture." This is the sure way to a cliché! An actor does not mechanically repeat a movement, but rather repeats the motivation, that causes the physical response. This process is never ending. *Acting is not a question of repeating, but of constant refinding.*

Techniques to Aid the Actor in Finding a Character

A complex character is a combination of many things. His physicality, his emotions, his thoughts and ideas—all are interwoven and influenced by each other. In turn, they are influenced by the social and historical context in which they manifest themselves and to which they respond.

In the following pages I have listed various methods and techniques that will help the actor in his task of creating the three-dimensional character. Their usage will be referred to throughout the chapter.

OBSERVATION

Observation is a tool to aid the actor's imagination. Through observation, the actor will develop a sensitivity towards physicality that will allow him to know when to hold on to something he has found, and, at the same time, when to let go. The actor must watch how an individual behaves in specific situations; he must analyze what they do, and why they do what they are doing. What is his self-image? What is his age? What is his health? What are his reactions to externals such as heat and cold? What does he find comfortable? What is his mood? Is he delighted, fearful, tired? What has caused his mood? Most importantly, *how* do we know? How do different people behave in the same situation? The way one waits, sits, eats, sleeps, cooks, plays cards, watches television, dresses—all are reflections of emotional and social conditions.

The actor must always ask himself what makes people the way they are. He must not imitate but rather understand and on the basis of this understanding, create.

BUILDING THE PHYSICALITY OF A CHARACTER, LAYER BY LAYER

From a neutral position, the actor begins to build his character, paying special attention to his breathing. He must first locate a neutral inner rhythm, his character in inactivity. He will then begin to breathe in the age of his character, his health, his physicality—finding the consequence of all that the character has done or does with his body, including his work and his leisure. He can next expose the physical feelings he has found, to the externals—cold, heat, comfort—and find how his physicality will respond. He must discover his energy level, which will depend on who he is and what he has been doing. The actor will notice that "exhaustion" after running a race is a very different matter from the "exhaustion" that results in years of "mothering." Finally, he must consider his present "mood," and his primary tool here will be the "inner monologues." Only now is he ready to take this character into movement.

INNER MONOLOGUE

This simply refers to the acting technique of talking to oneself, much as people do, in real life, as they walk down the street. This is a wonderful way for the actor to concentrate on his character's most intimate being: his moods, his thoughts, his rhythm. "To talk to oneself is an emotive action...."(Barrault).[8]

ACTOR'S BUSINESS

This is a difficult concept because it so often refers to something that has been added on as an afterthought and not based on an organic process. "I'll give her a squint or hiccups," the actor thinks. What exactly do we mean when we say an actor finds a "wonderful bit of business"? For me, it implies the ability of the actor to identify a moment that feels very "right," and then to keep it, develop it, and focus the audience on it. But an actor must find these moments, these "bits," through the same process he has been using to discover everything else. They must come from somewhere, are a result of something, and seem to represent implicitly that moment. It is important that the actor is working with the sensitivity and clarity to recognize these moments, to sense them, and to be able to remove from them any excess clutter. He must be able to sustain these moments and to polish them. Perhaps an "actor's business" could be considered simply a moment that expresses the character's essence? Often this essence can be comic in nature and useful in creating the effect of distancing.

Mannerisms, too, are physical responses to specific circumstances particular to the character, e.g., fingernail biting or a nervous little cough. If the actor's body is a responsive one, mannerisms will find themselves seemingly emerging on their own.

A character's body *develops*—it is the actor's task to plunge into the work to discover its physicality and physical behavior.

MOTIVATED MOVEMENT

An actor must be very clear about the reason and cause for every movement. He must move only with clear objectives. He must uncover and nurture the dramatic conflicts, both inside and outside his character. In order to do this he must open himself to the situation. Action comes out of the situation. In turn, emotion follows action.

INNER RHYTHM

The inner rhythm of a character is the actor's music. It is the inter-actions of all the characters that create the rhythm of the piece. Such music must evolve from the whole and cannot simply be applied from the outside, as it usually is in dance.

To study inner rhythms is to sense, study, and develop the rhythm of abstract inner feelings. The actor must look closely at, and be able to recreate in great detail, the rhythms of animals, of the elements, etc. He must find the musicality in the working body. Marceau refers to "le mouvement que chante."

The skill of learning to listen to and recreate the rhythms of characters far from one's own experiences is the basis of physical character work. There is a whole gamut of influences that will create the inner rhythm of a given character in a given moment. The physicality that will emerge, be it explosive and angular or lyrical and rounded, will create the image the audience sees and understands. Inner rhythm is the key with which actors can develop three-dimensional characters based on their research, their observations, and their decisions.

The actor's need to speak should be no different from his need to move. All too often, however, the actor gets caught up in the rhythm of the "poetry of words" and misses the "poetry of the dramatic moment." Movement, sounds, and words are simply the expression of the actor's inner rhythm, emerging to the surface through his breath.

DRAMATIC VALUE OF A MOMENT

The dramatic value of a moment must be clear to the actor if he is to be able to focus his audience, and to guide them as they watch. What is of primary importance at a given moment? How can the actor help the audience to be clear? What are the techniques available to him?

DICTION OF MOVEMENT

The rules of diction: punctuation, stress, and articulation—all have a place in the study of an actor's movement. Language structure can be very helpful in understanding the process of achieving articulate physical expression. Decroux paralleled specific instances in speech and movement where such rules of structure reflect the same needs. He pointed out that the sigh in movement has a similar use to the comma in speech. A pause or stop following a series of movements is used in much the same way as the full stop. An explosive stop is like an exclamation point. A movement that withers away creates the illusion of indecisiveness, of questioning. A series of movements which comes to a clear conclusion is much like a sentence, or a series of words that conveys a thought. Both have beginnings, middles, and ends. In a sentence some words are more important and, therefore, more stressed than others. Not every movement is of equal dramatic value. Intensity and focus will be used, when needed, to accentuate our intentions. Monotony creates a lack of clarity, whether through words or movement.

PHYSICAL ESSENCE OF A CHARACTER

The actor must be in search of the gesture or word that will express the heart of the character at a given moment. Finding the essential means discarding the loose bits and safeguarding the whole.

THE DRAMATIC INTENT

In response to the intent of a given moment the actor will find the rhythms, designs, intensity, and focus of a given moment changing. New elements will be called upon to develop the new moment.

The Walk

The walk has been a prolonged study for all of those who are truly interested in the analysis and creation of physical character. It therefore deserves a few words on it alone. Decroux, Barrault, Lecoq, and the *Théâtre du mouvement*, to mention only a few, have spent years on the subject.

For the actor, the walk is simply an extension of everything a character is, i.e., what he does with his body, what his self-image is, and how his status and interactions with others manifest themselves.

The whole history and physicality of his body can be seen in the walk.

As in all movement, it is the breath that dictates the walk. What is it about someone's walk that seems to make them appear to be "always in a hurry," or, on the contrary, to be "laid back"? Much of the answer can be found in analyzing how the character breathes. The actor must not, however, start back to front and decide to adopt the image of an explosive character, simply because it would be interesting. There must be a process whereby the explosive quality comes from within the character, and indeed becomes the dominate focus. *One does not find the walk; One first finds the body—the person.* The walk will emerge.

Perhaps the best way to learn about walks is to observe. Watch, analyze, find the rhythm, the breath, but don't try to copy. What is specific about a particular walk? What leads? What has influenced the walk? How has the climate, or the character's age, mood, emotional state, his energy level, and health affected the walk? What is the difference between the walk of extreme old age and of a five-year-old? How do shoes, clothes, status, and self-image influence the walk? *What makes the body move the way it does?* Watch the role of the pelvis in the walk. How do gender differences affect the walk?

What makes a walk specific to a specific character? An understanding of the character's physicality, his need to move—where and in what situation—will define the walk. Where has the character come from and where will he be going? What surface has he been walking upon (e.g., mud or pavement), and how familiar is he with all these influences and circumstances, etc.?

By stylizing a walk we mean taking the reality and finding the essence of the movement. What is it that makes the walk unique, what we see and focus upon? In finding the essence we will find that which seems to create the physical identity of the character. We will look at how the character transfers his weight, how he moves from his knees, and how he uses his hips. We must analyze where the walk seems to begin. With which part of the body does the character seem to lead, from the chest, the pelvis, the feet, or the head?

The walk can give a person away, in spite of himself. An unidentified person approaches us. His walk immediately tells us a great deal about him. "...a man may be betrayed by his walk" (Barrault).[9]

Conclusion

Getting the best acting possible from a given dramatic situation is a process that must remain flexible. I have found that an actor should simply have at his fingertips as many methods and processes as possible. One may serve him at one point, another may unlock a block at another. At times there have been tendencies to hold on to "truths" about how to achieve an articulate actor. "The Method" was one of these tendencies. "Physical Theatre Training" based entirely on skills from circus, or street theatre is another. "Playfulness" beyond all else is yet a third example. Many of us, interested in popular forms, grabbed hold of the concept of "representation"—acting was not "showing an experience" or "being,"but rather "representing." Fair enough, but the results were often two-dimensional cartoon characters, limited, heavy on style, and inarticulate. Our productions did not look at all like those of the Berliner Ensemble or Dario Fo, which had managed to find all the complexities of the plays' contents and still be very essential and visually exciting. It took time to find how best we could achieve this representation. More often than not, we found the answer in the actual structure of the play or piece, rather than the actors' individual preparation.

The audience is watching circumstances in which characters function. The actor's primary task is to communicate the ideas of the piece. Form and style are there to serve the piece, and do not, in themselves, constitute theatre. Characters must be clear, must interact, must be credible. It is through process that these things can be achieved. Actors will make use of varying theatrical structures (such as "turning-out" to the audience or gestus work), but the initial process will be the same. Comprehension of a character must begin from an understanding of his everyday life. Its development will depend on where the character, in the piece, is heading.

In this chapter we have looked at processes that hopefully will help free an actor to discover and then adopt the physical body of the character he wishes to portray. The actor must not be limited by his own body, by his mannerisms, or by his own experiences. He must have a wealth of material to draw upon. We have seen this can be done through an understanding of the concept of "physical feeling"—the finding, sustaining, and recreating a physical feeling and the physical, muscular responses to these feelings. It is a method that permits these feelings to become visible by way of a responsive, sensitive body.

Imitation, however, never allows an actor to integrate the physicality of his character into his own body. Physical characterization remains an outside layer and is thus easily lost as the first physically difficult moment presents itself. How often we see the actor resorting to his own body, his own strength, as he carries someone down the stairs, or as he enters into a taxing "emotional" scene.

The well-trained actor should be able to move from farce to tragedy, with great freedom, finding the most articulate way possible to present the contents of his role.

Perhaps these thoughts aren't the answer to all texts or theatre situations all of the time. But they are to be taken for what they are—a means, a process to help actors make clear the whole—bit by bit.

3 | The Actor's Instrument

THIS CHAPTER LOOKS AT THE SPECIFIC qualities that permit the actor to be physically explicit, alive and articulate in the theatre space. Why, we ask ourselves, do some actors seem to physically "die" on stage in a moment of stillness? They flounder about helplessly, waiting for their "turn to move," depending on a word or gesture or costume to rescue them from ambiguity. Yet there are other actors who create characters with such physical clarity that there can be no doubt, at all times, who they are, what they are feeling, thinking, being. Some actors seem to have a body that works for them; others seem hopelessly trapped in their own!

In examining the process of preparing the actor's body, it is necessary to define, with care, the qualities that are specific to an actor's physical training. In what way does the actor's physical training differ from that of the dancer's, or the athlete's, or the activities of the person who keeps himself "fit"?

Decroux said that the body must be a "well-tuned resonator." What he meant by this was that all that is happening inside the body must resonate outwards, through every part of the body—the trunk, the limbs, the hands, the face, the eyes. Only a prepared body, sensitive and capable, will provide the actor with the physical possibilities to communicate and to make clear statements. The basis of an actor's craft is to make that which is happening inside visible to the audience. The body is his instrument.

In certain cultures it is exactly this physicalization of thoughts and emotions, of interactions and relationships, that is restricted, if not downright taboo. At best, feelings are hesitantly allowed to reveal themselves verbally. But an actor whose body is blocked in such a way is a silenced actor. The language of the actor is a physical one. It is through this language the actor's imagination and creativity will declare themselves.

The body must be prepared to project clearly, with precision and detail. Everything is seen and serves as part of the dramatic statement. The actor must be in control and be able to exercise choice. His language, like any language, has precise rules of diction and a grammar of physical expression, which are to be learned and mastered. Articulate bodies are more than fit bodies. To be useful to the actor, they must be instruments that can be relied upon; instruments that will respond and react. Much as the musician's instrument must be well-tuned and the painter's brushes be in excellent condition, so must the actor's body be prepared for creative work.

At first, the actor must learn to understand the possibilities of physical expression, and how to prepare himself for such work. "Everything is all right as long as you do it on purpose," Decroux used to say. But the actor must know what his choices are and at the same time have an instrument that will allow him to choose. He must at all times be responsible to the material and the public.

Only when an actor is clear about the possibilities of his work can he begin to be clear about the actual process involved: what such work entails. The physical actor's objective is not merely to be "fit" or be able to execute acrobatic feats with great aplomb. Rather, he must begin to identify the causes (the motor) of an action and become increasingly sensitive to the image or statement it provokes. Movement, rhythm, tensions, and energy—all become vehicles through which he can converse; they are his language.

Everything an actor does is seen and interpreted by the audience. Scratching one's nose or blowing the hair from one's eyes will carry with it a meaning to those watching.

If an actor is to be clear, so too must be the process of his training. An actor's physical training must respond to an actor's specific needs: (a) the actor must be in control of his instrument in the performance space and free to respond to the dramatic moment; and (b) the actor must be physically imaginative and articulate.

"The essential aspect of my work is articulation" (Decroux).[1] Each movement has a value and is done on purpose, as a result of the dramatic need. A fleeting gesture of the hand or a wondering of the eyes reflects a thought or emotion specific to the given moment. The physical manifestation of a moment must be precise and articulate.

It is an aligned, aware, balanced, coordinated, neutral, responsive body that will permit the actor to begin to execute and make use of his craft. As he learns to stand and walk, to be in control, to have presence, he is learning to be clear. He will gain the capability to work with detail and precision. Fitness will result, but it is not the goal.

This work assumes a commitment on the part of both the actor and the training program. There must be a commitment of time that is necessary for muscle knowledge and muscle memory, as well as a commitment to follow the classroom work into the performance space. One does not become a physically articulate actor simply by wishing for it or with a lot of sweat. It requires acquiring a specific skill. This implies, perhaps, a need to change a mentality often present in acting students, as well as in the heads of certain teachers/directors—away from the "sweat, slug it out and build up stamina" mentality, towards the education of an actor in his language of movement. No one doubts the need for an actor to work on his body. The confusion remains concerned with how this work should be approached.

An actor must understand not only how a body functions, but must, as well, understand the function of movement in the theatre space.

One must move away from such common misconceptions as "I'm happy with my body, so I'm free to act!," or "Why can't I just say what I have to say"? As the actor learns his craft, he will find ways and means to express himself that he probably never dreamed could be accessible to him. Only a well-tuned instrument can be responsive to the acting demands made upon it. A body doesn't just respond because the actors intentions are clear or well motivated, or the impulse is "true."

During the work, actors will need constant reminders of the link between classroom and performance space. One must never lose sight of the application of the work, what it serves. The mystery surrounding why one actor may be physically present and clear and another not must be broken down. The skill that will permit the actor to make use of his craft with confidence must be provided.

The Actor's Physical Language: Important Concepts in Preparing the Articulate Body

The neutral body, immobile, breathing, is ready to act; the elements of motion—rhythm, intensity, and design—are at its disposal. The theatre space is ready to come alive.

THE NEUTRAL—A BEGINNING

"I am," "I have presence," "I have weight," "I exist in space," "I am ready to act (move)"—this physical state we will call the "zero." We are describing the physical and emotional neutral. It is from this point that the actor will be free to build and discover. The neutral is the takeoff point and landing place for the actor

It is exactly that—a neutral body. The actor is immobile, breathing gently, weight somewhat forward, secretly relaxed. He is never collapsed, nor is there any excess tension. The actor has prepared his body. It is aligned, strong, coordinated—ready to respond. The actor is free from personal mannerisms, his own body and its habits. He is therefore free to create a physicality far removed from his own and able to listen, respond, and react in the manner of his character. *"An actor must take on the body of the character, and not the character take on the body of the actor"* (Decroux). Every part of his body is neutral, ready to reflect, not only through the eyes, but through the whole body, all that is happening inside.

By listening to inner rhythms, by responding physically to his impulses (always with an economy of movement), and by permitting the motor (the cause) of a movement to direct the movement to its conclusion, the actor will find the means to build from his neutral. However, without a properly prepared body, it is often exactly at the point of building the physicality of the character and moving into the physical action that the actor finds himself becoming lost. He "mumbles" physically his intentions and is unable to sustain that which he has created.

He will find himself returning to architectonic gesture, applying movements and gestures here and there, in hopes that they will correspond to or illustrate the character's intentions. When this happens, the actor should always return to his "zero," his neutral, and rebuild from there.

IMMOBILITY—."A LIVING IMMOBILITY"(DECROUX)

In neutral, the actor is immobile. An actor without skill finds stillness very difficult. He squirms, unable to sustain and express that which he has identified inside. Only when throwing himself about the space or when speaking lines does he feel as if he is doing something, or that he is being interesting. However, it is in stillness that the actor begins to create. He senses the inner rhythm through his breath. Through the breath the actor becomes and remains vibrant, alive, ready. It is when these moments cannot be sustained that the actor finds his body dying in the space. Character and motivation become lost. The actor becomes an empty shell, waiting for a piece of business or words that will offer him a lifeline into shallow, but safe, waters.

Slogans such as "action in inaction" or "action-packed stillness" are often used in the mime world. Their meaning is clear. The mime world, at its best, has long understood and used the power and clarity of stillness to focus its audience. But such a technique implies a prepared, breathing, concentrated actor, with clear intentions, permitting the action to be sustained in the inaction.

Stillness commands great power and authority in the theatre space. An actor must learn how to use it. Stillness gives clarity to relationships. It brings focus to a moment or rest to the end of a thought (much as a full stop does in diction). It gives the audience space in which to take in the process leading up to and causing an action; stillness permits the transitional moments to be seen.

Neutral, immobile, the actor breaths. As the prepared actor begins to create the physicality of his character, his body will follow the dictate of the breath. The breath is the reflection of the characters feelings and is often a clear response to his thoughts. The chest translates backwards in distrust or forward in anticipation. Eyes enlarge with excitement, the breath abated. The sigh, the gasp, the shallow breath all reflect the interior. In a skilled, responsive body, these feelings, both physical and emotional, will manifest themselves with precision and detail. In the trained body the impulse will manifest itself through tensions, vibrations, isolated movements, and rhythms and carry them through to their conclusions. A hesitant glance over the shoulder will be executed by a slight turn of the head and neck, and not a flinging about of half the body; the prepared body may spin in surprise as a reaction to a noise behind it, with great speed and tension and without falling on its face!

Breath expresses emotion. The slightest movement of the chest can betray all that is happening inside. One image that Decroux used that I find very useful, but which is often misunderstood, is the idea of the "nipples as eyes." One has just to look at an actor whose face is covered to discover the enormous clarity with which feelings are expressed through the chest. It is through the chest that all the subtleties of the interior become visible.

Gesture originates in the breath. Breath causes a movement. And it is the thoughts and feelings of the person or character that determine how the breath will manifest itself. The chest lifts, or droops, or retreats, and the rest of the body follows. The impulse is taken to its conclusion. There is no reason to "set" movement. A responsive body moves to the dictate of the dramatic moment.

THREE ELEMENTS OF MOVEMENT— THE BASIS OF THE ACTOR'S GRAMMAR

Decroux noted and defined three elements at the actor's disposal when using movement as his means of dramatic expression. As physical actors, we have the design, the intensity, and the rhythm of a movement or movements with which to work, in bringing our ideas to their visual theatrical form. It is important to understand how these elements may serve the actor and how they affect that which the audience sees and understands:

design: the line created in space, the aesthetic use of space
intensity: the amount of intensity given a moment or a
movement
rhythm: accents and lengths through which movements'
relationships are expressed

1. *Design* refers to the image created by the actor(s) in the space, and what the audience sees and understands by these images. The positioning of a body or bodies creates what I call a "stage picture," and it is through these theatrical images we communicate our specific ideas to the audience. The design in space can be either (a) movement starting from the inside; the result of emotion or thought that manifests itself through breath, continuing out through the extremities, and, unless blocked, continues to its end (not unlike a sentence); (b) a movement caused by an external action—for example, a shove, or a trip—that will often cause not only a physical reaction (falling) but an internal reaction as well (fear, pain, anger); or (c) movement that is architectonic; that is to say, is concerned with creating specific lines in space by external decisions or sources, dictated usually by an aesthetic use of the space (choreographed movement). Much dance falls into this category.

The design created by movement has both a narrative and aesthetic value. It can be however limiting and two-dimensional. It is through the intensity and rhythm with which the movement is executed that meaning and dramatic value are achieved. All movement can be analysed as a rotation, inclination, or translation, or some combination thereof. This is to say that all movement can be categorized as being an example of one of these possibilities. The movement can be composed of isolated movement (a combination of any of the isolated parts of the body) or the movement can be created by the total movement of the body, as in a block.

By isolated parts of the body, we mean movement on its own of the head, neck, chest, waist, and pelvis. The legs and arms are appendages of the torso. They can move independently in architectonic fashion or along with, and in response to, the movement of an adjacent part of the body. Or they can be a part of the total, by which we mean movement of the whole body as one unit.

The ability to isolate and move parts of the body at will, is an invaluable skill for the actor. It provides the actor with the control and physical freedom necessary to move with economy and to discard all excess. It is exactly this skill that will enable the actor to respond in an articulate manner to internal or external stimuli.

If such analysis appears mechanical to the young actor, we must remind him that, as both instrument and artist, the actor must have an instrument that is prepared to respond to the demands of creating theatre. Through design the outline of the dramatic image is created.

2. *Intensity* refers to the level of tension a movement uses in conveying a theatrical moment. It is the primary means we have to focus the audience on what we deem important. In speech, not every word in a sentence is of equal importance; nor in theatre is everything, every image, of equal dramatic value. We do not speak one word at a time, each with equal stress, nor do we move in such a monotonous manner. The more intense a movement, the greater dramatic importance it will have. Greater, too, will be the emphasis on the given moment in which it is happening.

Much like the close-up in film, intensity forces the audience to look at the specific. For example, if there is one relaxed hand and one tense hand, the tense hand will dramatically dominate, and that is where the audience will be focused.

Intensity replaces time.

Effort is shown through intensity.

Quickness and intensity results in the compression of time.

Repeated, intense rhythm can give feeling of mass heartbeat—the feeling of the mob, for example.

Intensity is the means by which the actor directs the audience's attention.

3. *Rhythm* is the speed at which a movement is executed. Rhythm controls the level at which the audience will take in an action. An audience's understanding and clarity will differ depending on whether it has been offered a fleeting glimpse or a long, focused stare. It will help dictate what the audience sees and in what detail.

Highly stylized theatre will usually use non-natural rhythm as a means to get to the essence of a movement.

For the actor, rhythm is dictated by dramatic need, not a specific beat or music. Through rhythm the actor controls how the audience looks upon a specific dramatic event. A dramatic situation, presented in long lyrical movement will leave a very different impression in the minds of the audience than the same situation revealed through a series of explosions.

THE BODY IN SPACE—USING THE THEATRICAL SPACE TO MAKE CLEAR DRAMATIC STATEMENTS

When speaking of creating the stage picture we mean simply the actor's use of his physicality as a means to create a theatre image. From this image the audience will arrive at certain understandings and draw its conclusions. The actor must be aware of a variety of techniques at his disposal and at the same time be capable of making use of these techniques. Not only must the actor have made clear decisions, and be in physical control of both himself and the space, he must, as well, be conscious of what it is the audience will see and understand by the image he has created. The actor's control of his physicality is what will make this work possible. "Truth," or the moment "working" for the actors, is not enough! Lines in space communicate specific ideas and specific relationships and are based on shared, learned understandings. The slightest change in image can easily change the audiences perception of a given moment. An actor can know, for example, that the drama in a particular scene requires the audience to be focused on his character. However, if he is hidden in the rear of the stage, and two powerful figures are upstage, the importance of that dramatic moment will be lost.

Three people in the stage space may be of equal significance and consequence to the scene; but the moment one actor turns his back on one of these characters in order to speak to the other, they are no longer of equal dramatic value in the space.

Many things can happen to an image given the slightest change in the use of what I call the "lines of space." For example, an audience's understanding of an action will be determined by whether the action is carried out in a direct line, facing the audience or on an oblique line, using the diagonal. Proximity, (how close the characters are to one another) and attention (where they are looking) will influence how the audience interprets a relationship. How the weight of an actor is placed will give an actor or a moment great dignity (forward weight) or a comic nuance (backward weight). All these techniques are part of the actor's language and must find a place in his training.

Many stage conventions are based on the audience's cultural understanding of the theatre space and what they believe can happen or is allowed to happen in that space. All actors must take this into consideration and know when and how to make use of these conventions, either by adopting or rejecting them. The stage space allows for a heightened awareness and acceptability of nonreality. The use of sets (windows, doors, etc.), stage falls, walks, compressed space, or time are all stage conventions creating illusions that may or may not be readily acceptable to the audience.

The actor will need to find a way technically to sustain, night after night, in new spaces of differing dimensions, differing shapes, and differing proximity to audience all that he has found through the process of rehearsal and previous performance. The same ideas must be conveyed through the same rhythms, tensions, designs. The actor depends on his physical awareness to make this possible.

NATURAL HARMONY AND MUSCLE MEMORY—MAINTAINING THE NATURAL IN THE ARTIFICIAL SITUATION

Movement that is natural and relaxed under natural circumstances is often lost by the actor in his artificial situation. When people walk, for example, they, more or less naturally, swing their arms in harmonic opposition to their leg movements. In the stage space there seems to be a tendency for such harmonious movement to disappear. Many actors end up walking with a swagger reminiscent of a New York cop or street tough.

The actor must study the essence of natural harmony and rhythm; a process of discovery made possible by a new level of awareness of human motor responses. Relaxation along with the control and use of energy and tension will be at the basis of this study.

We want a body that is free, aware, strong, aligned, flexible, coordinated, and ready to fulfil an actor's needs. It must be a creative, sensitive, responsive, a live tool. The methods to achieve this are varied but there is no way to avoid the need for or towards the process involved.

The Process: Achieving the Concept of the Physically Articulate Actor

THE WARM-UP—A MEANS TO GET THE BODY WARM, WORKING, AND RESPONSIVE

The warm-up serves a very specific function, often misunderstood by both actors and directors. It involves a *method* to maintain the physical instrument, but does not necessarily maintain the level of physical skill an actor may have already acquired. It is not a physical training in itself, but rather a partial maintenance program; a method designed to permit the actor to prepare the body for work, and to avoid injury. It must not be expected to replace a training program, nor should actors expect or be expected to maintain or develop physically simply by warming up. At the same time, its proper function is one of uppermost importance in an actor's work, and any training program must be responsible for teaching how this work should be approached.

It is very important that actors know how to warm up, both in an isolated situation and when leading or otherwise participating in a group. If done improperly, the work serves to no avail, or worse yet, works to the detriment of the actor. Often an actor's principle goal in warming up seems to be working up "sweat." Injury often is the result of such fast, sloppy work; meanwhile, the necessary work for careful self-awareness and detail becomes lost.

The warming-up process must involve warming up parts of the body, bit by bit, always working correctly and in great detail. The goal is to achieve a body prepared for an actor's work. There are correct and incorrect ways to work: a foot brush serves little or no importance if the foot isn't caressing the floor, each muscle working to its full extent; body swings incorporating deep knee bends can be absolutely harmful if the knees are not first well warmed-up or if the knees are allowed to turn in.

There must be a constant awareness of relaxation while working. The actor must be working with the least possible tension and energy needed to execute the movement—there must be no over exertion in order to "achieve" ("further, further," "faster, faster," "more, more"!). Relaxed muscles stretch well and contracted ones rip.

Nor are we speaking of a "regime" or repeated movements, which after a time tend to be done automatically and therefore no longer serve their purpose in preparing an aware, thinking body. The body needs to learn to "think" physically. There must always be an insistence in every warm-up on thinking about and analyzing a movement—what does this exercise serve and why?

Actors need to understand why they do what they do, and with this knowledge, use a movement as a point of departure. Movements must always be new and unfamiliar to make the body think and respond. At the same time, the exercises must be consistently addressing the constant "problems" facing the actors such as the warming-up of joints, and the preparing for the proper use of flexibility and strength.

In using a warm-up, actors must understand the physical need for a working order. They must know which movements prepare for and therefore permit the following set of movements. They must learn how to develop a warm up in a creative manner, and be able to lead or teach others in the work. At the same time they must have an accurate assessment of their own personal body "problems" and pay special attention to these.

As the body warms up, so too must the actor within the body. This is why individual actors, warming up by themselves, are only partially preparing themselves for the work ahead. Warm-ups should be done with the whole company; as the body becomes prepared, the actors are becoming alert, sensitive, responsive and open to the space and others in the space. All warm-up sessions should end with exercises that address specific needs.

What is the minimal warm-up? A warm-up must include:

Part A

1. Zero—the neutral

2. Gentle stretches, incorporating the total body; an awakening of the muscles

3. Stretches examining the relationship of one part of the body to another—paying special attention to back and joints

4. Knees, ankles, hips—gently warming them up

5. More demanding stretches for the total body, concentrating on movement in all directions—up, down; forward, backwards; to both sides

6. Deep knee bends, done slowly, first in a turned-out position, and only afterwards done in a parallel position if needed

7. Exercises using large movements of the total body; exercises for isolated movements and coordination, weight transfer, etc.

8. Stretch combinations, both long and wide that incorporate weight transfer, speed w/balance, and space

The Part A warm-up should be followed by floor work.

Part B

1. Hand stretches

2. Back work

3. Pelvis, leg stretches

4. Torso, stomach, more back

5. Relaxation

6. Relaxation in stretch (yoga)

Forty-five minutes should be allotted for a proper warm-up. Part A can be completed in twenty to thirty minutes.

A BASIC VOCABULARY—DEFINING THE COMPONENTS OF AN ACTOR'S PHYSICAL TRAINING PROGRAM, WHICH WILL INCLUDE:

Alignment—the analysis of an individual body and the relationship of each part to the whole.

In the study of alignment one will need to discover the sources of a body's tendencies, tensions, and weaknesses. The body must be placed, bit by bit, to form a straight, neutral, free instrument; one which is able to breathe, to balance, to move in a responsive, logical manner.

Back—a principle source of corporeal expression.

Emotion is reflected through breath, and it is precisely the vertebrae that permit this emotion to become visible to the outside. All too often actors seem dead from the neck down. The back is one of the most blocked, unused, unresponsive parts of the body, simply because it is physically not free to be articulate. Our weak backs are a result of an age when people spend much of their life sitting down. Little in our everyday life prepares our backs for the life of an actor.

Back work must include work on each vertebra, *carefully*, one by one. We will be looking for supple, strong backs, able to support the head and the torso and to free the limbs. It is a weight and a task almost too great for the human back. The work will involve learning how to use the back properly, aware of its weaknesses and strengths. Actors will need strong backs if they are to avoid injury.

All movements, unless architectonic, begin with the chest or head. The limbs extend the action, and it is the back that will allow this extension to happen.

Breath—dictates how a movement will manifest itself.

All exercise, beginning with the warm-up and carrying on through the rest of the physical training, must be conscious of the nascence of a movement. A movement must begin from the inside and, through the breath, extends outwards. If one moves without the breath as the source, the movement becomes robotic. It is through aware, controlled breathing that one achieves the relaxation necessary to move and speak in a responsive, vibrant manner.

As emotion dictates the breath, the tension and rhythm in the breath will dictate how the body responds physically. A gasp will result in an explosive movement; a sigh, in a long, lyrical movement. An awareness of the motor of a movement is essential. How a movement begins is how it will extend and how it will end.

Coordination—the ability to move parts of the body in a responsive, responsible manner, in relationship to their total physical design.

Whether the movement is imposed through architectonic design or whether an extension of an internal source, the body must be expected to react in harmonious fashion.

Counterweights—the basis and study of push and pull movements.

It is through the understanding and study of counterweights that we can analyze and reproduce work movements. By creating resistance in space, through the technique of counterweights, actors can create the illusion of weight.

Diction in movement—achieving clarity in movement or speech through the understanding and use of linguistic structure (refer to Chapter Two).

Elements—the intensity, rhythm, and design of a movement.

Energy—must be seen in the context of its specific dramatic use in the theatre space.

The level of energy in the performance space brings a specific dramatic value to a given situation and is in direct response to the level of tension reflected in that moment. There is a need to demystify "energy" and to reject the idea that energy is something an actor brings to the space from nowhere and regardless of the dramatic moment. Energy must originate from inside and be directed as it emerges. All too often the audience is attacked by hysterical, tense, wide-eyed images and given no space to receive or reflect. The actors' need to have the personal energy to achieve and sustain the work at hand is different from the use of energy as an actor's tool, and must be considered in a different context. Often they are hopelessly muddled. The director will demand of an actor more energy. But, ignorant of an actor's resources, he will encourage hyped-up activity, and lose the energy that should come forth as the result of the dramatic moment.

For example, explosive energy doesn't just happen. It is in response to the dramatic moment and is simply one way the energy may be released. An explosion is not, like fireworks, and end in itself. How it is released depends on the physicality of the character involved and will signify to the audience a dramatic direction.

Inner rhythm—from whence a movement originates, and which can only be reflected by an aware and responsive body (refer to Chapter Two).

Isolated movement—the ability to isolate parts of the body and specific muscles.

Through this sort of physical control, the actor is able to create the clarity of image necessary for the audience to see that which is intended. Isolated movement permits the actor to be free of all excess, to work with economy. If "everything is all right as long as it is done on purpose" (Decroux), it is exactly this skill that will give the actor freedom. The actor will look at all the possibilities of movement—the rotation, the inclination, the translation—and the image he creates, through the use of the isolated part (e.g., a turn or rotation of the head) or the whole (e.g., a turn or rotation of the whole body) with different levels of intensity and rhythm.

Relaxation—the ability to control the level of tension.

Thought must be given to the difference between the use of relaxation as a method to prepare an actor's body and the relaxation of the prepared body of the actor who is ready to act. In movement work we will be concerned with the concept of a "secret relaxation" (Decroux) as opposed to the collapsed body of the totally relaxed person. As the actor begins to work, there must be no obvious state of relaxation nor is there any excess tension. Neutral, the body is simply ready to move. This implies a secret relaxation. Muscles must be relaxed in order to stretch, yet not tear. Nor can one move in an explosive manner from a point of high tension. Again, we are speaking about an actor's physical control, his ability to make use of relaxation while still being firmly present; grounded, never floating; he is alive, ready to act.

Self-awareness—the ability of the actor to be aware, through physical feeling and the "third eye", of the picture he is creating in the theatre space.

The actor must be in control of the image he is creating or helping to create in the theatre space. Aware of what the audience is seeing, he must be responsive to them as well as to all that is happening in the space about him.

This is one of the most confusing concepts for the young actor. Concentrating on identifying and fulfilling physical impulses that are in direct response to the dramatic moment, the idea of always having a third eye on the audience seems to be in direct contradiction to all else he is trying to do. The key to this problem is found in the rehearsal process, where not everything happens a once. The actor, quite organically will discover impulses and with a heightened awareness of the space be able to develop them.

The dramatic space—the performance space must be defined and redefined; it is an artificial space, one created for dramatic use.

The actor must have a keen awareness of himself in the theatre space as well as the interactions and relationships with others in that space. The actor has the responsibility to make clear and develop these relationships.

He must understand stage techniques and conventions and be able to make use of them while still retaining all the skills that will make his performance credible. In creating the theatrical illusion the actor must be able to use techniques such as lines in space (i.e., direct or diagonal), proximity, and focus to convey his ideas in a clear manner, always aware of what it is the audience sees and understands.

Strength—the need for physical strength in supple, stretched muscles.

An actor must learn to use the minimum amount of strength necessary to achieve the dramatic moment. Therefore, when we speak of the need for an actor to be strong, we are not speaking of the blocked, contracted muscles and inflexible strength often associated with certain sports and weight training. An actor's physical training must insist on contracting and stretching muscles equally, in a systematic fashion. Certain other physical training programs work from the same perspective, such as swimming, and the ballet barre.

Stretch—flexibility and suppleness of strong muscles.

Transfer and placement of weight—creating theatrical illusion.

> The actor must be able to maintain balance while moving through space. He will be responding to the dramatic cause of the movement that may involve difficult transfers of weight and change in direction, not to mention split-second timing. He must use his eyes, have strong vertical muscle around his waist, and strong flexible feet, if he is to succeed. He must be able to move and stop precisely ("on a dime") and never allow himself to "trip out" with an emotional or physical feeling. Rather, he must be aware of the space and his weight in that space at all times.

Trust exercises—ensemble work requires knowledge of, and trust in the ability of others .

> Just "loving" someone or giving one's weight fearlessly is not enough. There is a need for all parties to know *how* to work. Techniques of support and balance must be a part of all training. We must be very clear that we are not talking about blind, fearless trust, but rather a thorough understanding of the physical possibilities of one another in the space, and the use of these possibilities to take the dramatic impulse to its conclusion. An actor must earn the trust of his colleagues.

Physical Turnout—there must be an analysis of both the aesthetic and practical purpose and use of turnout for the actor.

> The aesthetic purpose concerns the design created in space and the understanding of specific cultures concerning what is attractive or acceptable to that society. For example, in some cultures, a turnout is considered altruistic, attractive, open; while a turned-in position or gesture appears closed, egotistical, or clumsy. Other cultures may have differing interpretations of these same lines in space.

> The practical purpose concerns balance and freedom of movement. With the weight placed over the inside of the arch of the foot, the actor is stronger and more in control. Any transfer of weight, or change in direction; any movement through space, be it forward, sideways, or backward; stopping and balancing of all types will require the use of turnout.

The Walk—consists of a series of falls, a series of transfers of weight, which permit people to "stride" (Decroux) as their means of moving from one place to another.

> The speed, the intensity, and how the body responds to the transfer of weight are the result of the specific physicality of the character. The actor must take into consideration the veritable multitude of internal and external influences that determine a person's walk, (refer to Chapter Two).

For all the physical "tools of the trade" described above there are specific exercises. Samples of these are provided in the Appendices.

THE ACTOR'S PHYSICAL TECHNICAL SKILL— DEPENDABLE AND INVISIBLE

Physical skills provide the actor with the means through which he may express his ideas and thoughts in a clear, visual, theatrical manner.

In other performance arts the level of skill may almost fulfill an end in itself, e.g.,the thirty-two perfectly executed fouettes in ballet or the wonder aroused by the number of twists in a circus tumbling event. But the actor's means of expression, through which he creates his illusion, not only must remain invisible; they are, in themselves, important only in serving to clarify and articulate the objective of the theatre work.

A stumble in the theatre space is useful only if the audience is clear who the character is and under what circumstances the fall occurs. Out of context, the technique in itself serves no purpose. If the audience becomes aware of, and perhaps impressed by, the cleverness involved in creating a theatrical illusion, the dramatic moment becomes lost. The audience must be free to react and think about what a fall down the stairs signifies, and not how it was executed.

An actor's body must be open and responsive to all the influences, outside and inside, that cause him to react physically. The mechanics of an action, such as a trip or fall, must be automatic. The physicality of the character must be so familiar, so integrated into the actor's work, that the physical action (and the technique which permits the action) is simply an extension of a character's physicality.

An actor's physical performance skill allows him to create the illusion of reality or the essence of reality. It must be, however, his acting skill that dominates. Performance techniques are an intricate part of the actor's craft, supporting the demands of the acting. Without them, he is a limited, trapped actor, no matter how innately brilliant. The actor brings to his instrument his objectives, his intentions, his physical actions. The physically aware instrument will respond appropriately to these demands.

An actor must never be seen to anticipate an action. The audience, in fact, must be caught unawares, if not by the action, by the thought it provokes.

The skillful, free body, aware and in control of an actor's physical techniques, will, when integrated with acting skills, provide the means of expression. This is the right of every imaginative, conscientious actor.

An actor must be able to depend on his "tools" and be committed to the time necessary to achieve a skill. As an adult, one simply walks and no longer thinks about the process involved. But the toddler must work hard not to fall over. Learning to walk takes time. So do all physical skills. An actor must be given the time to develop these skills. There is no mystery why one actor can dash up the stairs and with equal ease fall down them again all the while, free to follow his dramatic impulse. He is simply an actor whose skills are serving him well.

Conclusion

After stillness in the empty space, the actor enters, walks, sits, reacts, makes a statement, exits. This is what movement training must address. We are not speaking about the ability to fly across the room. Nor is it a question of motion per se. The actor's concern is to interest and engage the audience through visual clarity.

An actor must develop a vocabulary, a grammar of movement, not a "technique." He must have the ability to produce clear, dramatic statements. I believe this to be the primary motivation behind Decroux's research.

The body must be trained. There is no mystery. Body work must not be treated as a casual supplement to an actor's training nor be confused with other physical performance skills. Thought must be given to the process. Many of today's tendencies in the physical training of the actor appear not to address the actor's specific needs. All too often we see energy simply thrown about. High energy, first and foremost, along with stamina building masquerades as movement training. Such work is not useful. It does not lead to the awareness, identification, and sustaining of physical feelings, which in turn will lead to physical clarity. Even in radio or television work the necessity of this sort of physical awareness cannot be ignored, for it is through a responsive body that an actors' sounds and words emerge. Nor is the aligned, fit person, in himself a good actor. An actor must learn to make use of his body. Detail, concentration, and precision must provide the basis for this work.

There has been a certain amount of confusion concerning the importance of a positive body image for an actor's work. "I like my body" or "I feel good in myself," young actors often assure me! This is hardly a bad thing but may be irrelevant to an actors needs. Certainly it is not the goal of an actor's physical training. It is even possible (and I have known many cases where this has been true) to find very good physical actors who don't like their bodies—but could they use them!

"The body must be ready and sensitive." (Brook).[2] One must be clear about this goal and then make a commitment to the time and process involved. The body and acting work must happen simultaneously. As the work develops, each greatly influences the other. The fully responsive body is there to express accurately the actor's intentions. It is important that movement work is never seen simply as a classroom activity or an entity in itself.

4 | Creating Theatre

THEATRE, WHEN SUCCESSFUL, is vital, articulate, and, above all, relevant to those watching. The pictures in the stage space reflect the social and cultural demands and restrictions of a specific historical time. It is in reaction and response to such influences, that theatre reaches out to its public.

The creating of theatre is a collaborative process, requiring the active responsibility of all those involved. This chapter is concerned with the creative actor and his relationship to this process. We are considering here the articulate actor, with an articulate instrument, and with ideas to communicate. All three elements are necessary to the actor. One is useless without the others. This chapter isn't concerned with "how to devise," but rather with looking at methods that will help prepare the actor to assume these responsibilities. The artist has long struggled to find a means to understand, to grasp, and to represent the society in which he works. The actor's task is no different.

Creating Images and Statements

The very nature of theatre is to construct, and then present to the public, interactions and relationships of people and situations. These dramatic moments are not read about, nor discussed; rather they are visually presented. Theatre workers create and interpret through dramatic, and therefore physical, means a dramaturgy that will permit the audience to see what they have seen a thousand times before, in a new light and with a new understanding. In an interview with a film magazine in the 1970s, Joseph Losey said something to the extent that all stories have been told. It is the manner in which they are told that is important. In creating theatre there are choices, and it is the responsibility of the theatre workers to make the best choice possible for the particular theatre project at hand. Theatre provides a structure in which life is pared down, permitting us to perceive and express the essential. There are many ways to do this, but at the basis must be the understanding that the reality of the theatre space is a different reality from that of real life. There is a different sense of space and of time. Theatre has its own, artificial reality, which will be seen from a distance. "The attempt to imitate nature by means of the artificial..." (Barrault).[1] I find this thought especially important in understanding why improvisation, though often apparently "successful" in the first instance, is never visually or theatrically complete in itself. One cannot avoid the difficult process of selection: the long struggle of discarding and developing.

Theatre workers must make the audience look at the familiar in a new, unfamiliar way. Everyday life is presented from a point of view. The ordinary takes on a distance and becomes seen from a new perspective. How this is done is what I mean by dramaturgy.

Actors create situations and images as well as characters. Their work stimulates the audience to examine these situations. Writers, actors, directors, designers, movement directors, and choreographers must all find a way to work and create together. Nothing is done in isolation. The responsibility for the work presented in the performance space is a shared one.

The Roles and Responsibilities
of Theatre Workers

It is important never to lose sight of the interaction between all those involved in the creation of a theatre work. This team of theatre workers must try to define their roles, and analyze why in the past these roles have been defined in the way they have. The team's goal will be to create a finished, truly collective work, representing the best ability of all those involved. Perhaps such theatre will require a new sort of actor as well as a new sort of director and writer. Every person involved must be a part of the whole, working, not for individual performance but *actively* responsible to the collective conception.

The problem theatre workers face is to present their statement clearly. This implies a clarity by all concerned as to what the performance is about: why and for whom this performance will exist. What is the purpose behind the creating of the theatre work? By posing such a question as a starting point, the theatre workers have an entry into the work at hand. As their work takes shape, the answer will begin to emerge with clarity, and more questions will surface. The various roles of each theatre worker involved in this struggle must be defined and in many cases redefined.

Too often the director has been seem as a "leader," to whom the actor either responds or rejects. A battle of individuals, each defending his/her territory, results. The concept of creating a theatre work through the efforts of a team is lost. The director must give a great deal of attention to the various methods at his disposal that will enable the team to achieve the desired performance. In his role as *enabler*, it will be the director's task to help get the best, clearest performance possible from the actors. The director must be able to pose questions and identify problems as they evolve organically from the rehearsal process. He is not imposing answers to preconceived questions, but rather responding to the offers of his colleagues. This implies a sensitive understanding of the actor's working process. Theatre workers must learn to be flexible to the demands of the theatre piece, and be able to employ methods applicable to these demands.

The relationship of the director to the actor is often one of the third eye. This gives the actor freedom to experiment but requires the actor to have trust in the director as a person flexible and responsive to an actor's resources. The director's role is not that of an acting coach but as a third eye in a position to help the actors find the economy and essence of their expression. As a third eye, the director is responsible for keeping the parts of the whole together—catching bits as they stray off target, guarding carefully all that is useful. This is not the role of policeman, nor should the director's word be seen to be the "final word," but rather a reflection of a specific responsibility on the part of the director.

When this mutual responsibility is ignored, the result is a theatre work encompassing a wild variety of styles and a great unevenness in performance. Directors, actors, and designers must, in the process of working "on the floor," be able to discuss, add, throw out, change, and never be bound to predetermined ideas and decisions. This is what we mean by flexible! There must be continual space given to the struggle and search for the best means possible to achieve the goals of the collective whole.

This division of actor from director (as well as other theatre-workers from each other, such as the frequently forgotten writer), often found in today's theatre, manifests itself through a sort of hierarchial system and can only be said to be holding back a great many possibilities in theatre development. Such a division results in a real lack of generosity between the actor and director that forces them into either non-productive conflict or non-creative submissiveness. Roles must be defined so that directors do not impose, nor actors become puppets. On the other side of the coin, theatre must not become a vehicle for tour de force acting. I should like to see a great deal of attention given to this schism, and methods developed to bring the collaborative process to the forefront. Certainly one of the best places to do this would be in the training programs.

Collaborative theatre requires skills on the part of the actors, directors, writers, technicians, and designers in devising and creating theatre. When confident about *how* to struggle towards collective responsibility in creating theatre, the need that the habitual hierarchy has traditionally fulfilled should vanish.

In discussing the roles of theatre workers in contemporary theatre, it is necessary to look back through history and analyze cultural differences in order to discover just how and why relationships between theatre workers have developed as they have. On this basis, decisions of where theatre is to go from here can be made.

Ways must be found to prepare theatre workers for a theatre of devising and creating theatre pieces, as well as for the working and reworking of texts. Such methods will need to be applied to, and follow, a clear company conception about the work. Collective decisions must be made concerning how the work will be presented. The responsibilities of the actor, the director, the writer, and the designer and, perhaps most important, the audience must be defined and brought up to date with the role of contemporary theatre in a contemporary society. The collective responsibility of the theatre team requires a mutual and thorough understanding of the working methods available to each of the company members. Their work is irrevocably linked: they enable one another to imagine, to discover, to shape, to reorganize, and to sustain. Only then can we really speak of ensemble theatre: theatre workers working together in their art form to express clear statements on humanity, through humor, conflict, harmony, joy, and sorrow.

Content, Form, and Style: The Choice

In order to present their ideas clearly, theatre workers will need to search for a common approach and a common language. Thinking as a closely knit unit about their work, they will need to grasp how the contents of the work will be perceived and understood by their audience. Cultural statements come out of and go into social situations. The reasons for wanting to express the ideas through theatre, along with the relationship of the contents to the audience, will help determine how the work is conceived and eventually put in the theatre space. Through movement and sound the actors must find the best way to achieve this goal. Successful communication is of primary importance.

Skilled theatre workers have a *choice*. They should not be limited by style or mode of presentation, but rather they should be free to choose that which is best suited to the work at hand. An acting "method" or "technique" (a language) should not imply a style in itself. I think here of Decroux and Stanislavski, whose teaching methods have often been interpreted, I believe incorrectly, as a style of acting. Nor does a theatre form (commedia, mime, forum theatre) dictate, necessarily, a style. Many theatre forms have changed their style by a little or a lot as they have developed or as the historical situations have changed. Theatre style refers simply to how a statement is made theatrically—through which theatrical means an idea is presented. Styles have been created and used with very clear intentions, reflecting specific cultures and historical moments. Many styles are complex, consisting of specific skills and requiring highly developed craft and much study. But the goal is the same: that of finding the best way possible to make accessible theatrically the contents of the work to an audience.

As situations and audiences change, the contents may require new and different means of presentation. Nowhere can this be seen more clearly than in the work of Bertolt Brecht, who reworked material in quite different ways depending on differing audiences, in differing social and political situations. (Such were his productions of "Arturo Ui"). In another vein, we have all seen examples of how a work or text can be totally modified, its meaning changed, simply by a mode of presentation other than what was intended. Again Brecht comes to mind when we think of the original American translation and production of "Three Penny Opera." This production managed to make a sentimental, colorful, American musical comedy out of the work!

The key word here is *choice*. The entire theatre team must make clear decisions based on the reason the work is to exist, from whom and for whom. Choosing a style, designed to be a theatrical "tour de force," without regard for or responsibility to the content or audience, is venturing on dangerous ground, and into which many companies sink. An actor's technique should encompass complete control of his instrument, allowing him both at a physical and emotional level the freedom to move from theatre form to theatre form, from style to style, dictated to only by the work at hand. The choice will be influenced by a great many things, including the social, aesthetic, and cultural backgrounds of both audience and theatre workers. Specific target audiences and performance spaces will also influence the decision.

It is simply a question of to whom we are speaking and why. The objectives of the performance are as much a part of the creative process for the actor as is the task of bringing the work alive in the performance space.

If we accept that theatre is, in itself, artificial, and one cannot within its' restrictions recreate reality, we can then accept that any method of presentation is a result of the theatre workers' imagination and ability to create. This is true whether we are speaking of an attempt to recreate reality or to present complex, often abstract thoughts. Nonrealistic image is often a most efficient way to communicate. An essential theatre, perhaps symbolic in nature, can achieve images that are more direct than everyday pictures or words or attempts to replay real life. The choice is there. Just as the writer may write a poem or an essay, so may the theatre worker choose how he will present his ideas. A theatre work does not present society but rather reflects upon it. Its value will depend on the artist's understanding and presentation. Styles are not simply applied but come out of the artist's need to communicate with clarity. Stylizing involves taking a reality and emphasizing, in one manner or another, its essence. Such economy often leads to the creation of focused expression.

"...abandon naturalism, and yet remain true...." (Barrault).[2]

"...stylization should not remove the natural element, but heighten it" (Brecht).[3]

All is not equal. Some styles will be more relevant than others. Styles have developed for reasons and are reflective of many things. All this must be taken into consideration when creating theatre.

John Berger speaking on selection in "Art and Revolution" commented, "We must distinguish between naturalism and realism. Naturalism is unselective or rather is selective only in order to present with maximum credibility the immediate scene."[4]

I find this helpful to the actor. Realizing the need to be selective leads precisely to finding the whole and paring it down.

There are many ways and many techniques to achieve this clarity. Contradiction, contrast, distancing—all are techniques to be discussed and used. Careful decisions are needed throughout. A piece of music may be used, for example, in contrast to or in correspondence with a dramatic moment. Very different statements will result depending on how a technique is used. This should be part of the rehearsal discovery.

Where to Begin: Creating Theatre in the Space

Theatre workers are in search of the best approach to present the material and ideas at hand. John Berger always reminds us that it takes skill to find and create the picture you want. In creating the theatre picture, all the components that make up the performance must come together. The smallest moment can greatly influence that which the audience sees or understands. Breath and focus can make all the difference. Visual and sound aids such as set, props, costumes, lighting, music and sound effects can help find the principle focus of the work. At the same time they are capable of distracting or totally changing the audience's understanding.

There are many ways to set about creating what will eventually take place in the theatre space. I would suggest, however, that working from a rigid preconception, developed in preproduction meetings, can result in a sort of creative rigor mortis. Theatre is a *vital* art form. Its creative process necessarily demands lively, dynamic interactions between the dramatic artists. In order to be successful, these creative interactions must be a part of the rehearsal process. Once the company has agreed to the overall ("super") objective for the work and made clear decisions concerning the relationship of the theatre work to the audience, creative development should be allowed to emerge in an almost organic manner. Certain rehearsal techniques will be more successful with certain material or dramaturgical structures than others. There is not a right way or wrong way to work. But it is important that the company has clarity and is able to recognize what it is looking for in order to develop its vision as the work evolves. Relationships between actors, directors, writers, and designers will also influence how a company will choose to work. Again, there are no hard and fast rules. But a company must have the skills that will permit them to *choose* their work methods. They must be able to distance themselves from the work and be able to analyze what is successful and what is not. They must have the freedom to explore and try, time and time again, new ideas and methods, always discovering. It is the company, as a whole, that will move the theatre piece forward, as a whole.

The question is how can the theatre space best be used to communicate to the audience the principle objective of the work. In creating the whole "picture," the company will need to work in large tableaux as well as with the minutest details. There will be searching, finding, clarifying, and then solving the questions that will arise in the process. Actors must be thought of as creators of images and not as interpreters of words within the director's or designer's "image". The stage picture emerges and is not imposed.

Exercises must be found that will allow the actors to recognize and then precisely define the interactions and dramatic moments that make up these images. Exercises are successful if they stimulate the actors imagination and assure that the action organically emerges as a result of its cause. With an unlocked imagination the actor will find himself free to move from one action to the next; the physicalization of the moment coming out of the dramatic situation. Preconceived or "set" patterns of movement often have disastrous consequences, as they come from nowhere and have nowhere to go. If movement in the stage space is not allowed to surface and develop, blocks in the creative process set in. The odd display of skill—a few dance steps or a slapstick stage fight—are often inserted and serve to illustrate the kind of bind in which theatre workers can find themselves.

The struggle during rehearsal is exactly that of not getting blocked, or rather how to keep the movement of the whole unfolding and developing. If the work does get "stuck," the question facing everyone is how to get "unstuck". There is a tendency for one of two things to happen: either the actors will bang their heads against the wall and forget to explore, or the company will permit this dead moment to remain, in hopes that it will go unnoticed. It is necessary to open up such a moment. There are many means to this end, but usually the process will involve the insistence on establishing the essence of the dramatic moment. From where does the moment get its breath? Where is the focus of the moment, the intensity? It is by working through such a process that the answers appear. As the actor's imagination responds and creates, the person in the role of the third eye, always observing, will be there to guide the actor. The actor is struggling to find the essential; the director is eliminating any excess. Together they must find clarity. Directors are as good as the actor's imagination, pulling out of him moments that are "almost" happening, crystallizing others, insisting upon and safeguarding still others. The director is in the position to see the whole, which in turn frees the actor to work for the moment. If things are going well, the actor's offers and responses will fulfil the objectives. A director's job is to see that it all fits together rehearsal after rehearsal, then night after night.

If things are not fitting together, it is up to the company as a collective whole to figure out the causes. This must be done with everyone "on their feet"—through work, through trial and error. If, for example, two actors continually are bumping into each other at one specific moment, the directors, actors, and perhaps the writer must face up to the fact that the action is a problem and that a solution must be found. But the solution must come out of the dramatic situation, taking into consideration the cause that resulted in the effect. Nothing must happen in isolation.

It is exactly this sense of process that is often found lacking in the work of the drop-in expert. "Brought in," the work of the choreographer, or dramaturge or musician is tacked on rather than extruded from the rehearsal process. The use of expertise "input" has often served as a way to help the actor to solve specific problems as they arise. But such expertise is only helpful if it is incorporated into the teaching or rehearsal process. Helping the creative imagination manifest itself clearly is possible when everyone involved is well acquainted with the work and in a position to view it as a whole. Problems and blocks evolve out of the work and must be considered from this perspective. The specialist, whether considering ideas (the dramaturge) or the execution of a movement (the movement director), must be there to assist the actor to achieve what he is after. This cannot help but imply an understanding and sensitivity to the process. These people must be a part of the team.

An actor's training, therefore, must be concerned with training team actors. As in the case of the musician, the dramatic artists must learn to listen and respond physically with their whole beings. As in the orchestra, theatre performance is the work of a collective body. Actors need each other and the rest of the team. Egoism can only confuse the work at hand.

How to Influence the Image: All Is Not Equal

There are many techniques that will enable the process of discovery during the rehearsal period. As the work progresses, each member of the company, working in his or her respective role, will be finding, defining, and refining. Physically, images begin to clarify and ideas begin to take on a theatrical shape. One idea will lead to another. "Ideas couple and have children," Decroux said. The struggle is to make the event, the action, clear, providing the audience with information that is never cluttered or confusing. "We must know all," Decroux said, from the point of view of the audience. Brecht insisted on knowing why a character was suffering.[5] The successful process will allow the statement or impression to develop fully. In this way, generalizing can be avoided. In the theatre, sloppy, ill-defined thoughts lead to picture clutter; complexities are lost and blurred pictures result.

The best way to approach the work will be dictated by content and by the target audience. At first there may seem to be a great deal of trial and error. But gradually the ideas and the context within which the work is happening will begin to define the approach and presentation. During this period, there are many things to be kept in mind. Most important must be *the constant realization that every-thing is seen, and therefore meaningful; but all is not equal.* What determines how an image is understood is the design, rhythm, and intensity with which it is presented. These elements are our language. A change in rhythm and intensity can completely change how an image is seen and understood. The result may be in total contradiction to the original concept.

All movements (actions) are defined by the circumstances and motivations from which they evolve. Actors, directors, etc. will work from the starting point of a realistic impulse and develop it towards its conclusion. We are not speaking here of personal impulses, but rather impulses caused by and coming out of the dramatic situation. How far to go? That, again, is a question of artistic judgement. All that is superfluous will be discarded; just enough will be shown to be clear. In fact, to be clear means showing just enough. Losey remembered that the thing that most irritated Brecht about English theatre was all the useless movement..."an empty kind of movement...."[6]

Decroux's methods of work involved stripping believable, real characters, in order to uncover their passion and their humanity. Through the essence of everyday reality the inner state or being could become visible. At the same time, the situation could become even more comprehensible and therefore more believable. Decroux valued humor, and perhaps most of all, passion, as a means to make the mundane action open to new interpretation and further understanding. We see in his work, for example, the hesitation before declared passion, or the inner monologue or dialogue that is in contradiction to the outward gesture.

Economy results from clear decisions. Each moment serves to provide a further understanding of a scene. In one scene the opening of a door may be the turning-point of the scene; in another it may simply serve as a detail that helps make the scene more explicit. Actions, such as arranging flowers, wrapping a scarf about one's throat, turning a door key, controlling stray strands of hair—all have specific dramatic value, which in turn will serve the idea and the audience.

If a scene has been approached with an image firmly fixed in the head of the actor or director, the task before them becomes one of motivating and activating this image—bringing this image physically alive and making it work. The inherent dangers of such a method are readily apparent if one keeps in mind that we are dealing with dramatic theatre, communicating ideas and not simply aesthetic phenomena. Actors create by responding. The physical image must have its beginning—somewhere. It must have a reason to be. It must be free to grow.

Actors and directors will add the detail necessary to give the moment its specific character. As the work proceeds, the third-eye (director) will be able to take from the physicalizer (actor), reorganizing and pruning the work as it evolves, steering it along its path towards clarity. The actor, for his part, must never lose sight of his character and actions in the context of the whole.

The exercises found in the appendix under three Model Workshops may help clarify this process. Books by Odin Theatre, Peter Brook, and Boal provide many more. Through improves and exercises the company begins to find the best way to work. Different ways of influencing an image will be explored and the one that serves the goal best will be used. Where to put the focus? How best to make use of language, sound, visual aids? In which style or with what music should the piece advance? These are questions to be solved in the interest of making clear, visual, theatrical statements.

Decroux spoke of condensing an idea in space and time. Perhaps this is yet another definition of gestus. Gestus must not be thought of as a single gesture or phrase, but rather an overall image (physical attitude) through which the audience recognizes the emotional and intellectual qualities of the character within the dramatic moment. When this is successful it is almost impossible to "carry along" an audience or to sentimentalize an idea. Gestus is "the essential attitude which underlies any phrase or speech" (Willett).[7] As a method, it is direct and encourages theatre workers to define their terms. Through economy, everything becomes essential and concentrated. The gestus emerges from the dramatic moment; this must not be forgotten. Before paring down a moment, it must first be considered in great detail.

The rhythm and intensity with which the design in space is executed will influence greatly what the audience does or doesn't see: what it knows and what it senses . In other words, it influences *how* the information will be received. When we speak of design, we mean the stage picture—how the actors are grouped, placed, distanced within the space. This should result in the physical manifestation of relationships: of character(s) to character(s), character(s) to situation(s), character(s) to idea(s), etc. *It is the physical organization of the dramatic moment.* Sometimes quite unexpected results occur. For example, it is always surprising how erotic a loving gesture across the space can be when compared to a passionate embrace of real contact. Think, too, how revealing a longing glance at the nape of a neck can be, in place of an elaborate, literary declaration of love.

Through rhythm and intensity a scene achieves its dramatic value; its significance. It is with these tools that we *focus* an audience, much as a close-up does in film. We have said that everything in the stage space is seen, but also that everything is not equal. In other words, the greater importance a moment or a gesture has to a scene, the more it will receive focus. Such accent can be placed in many ways. The techniques include, for example: a) *isolation*—"On a plain blue wall a single fly is noticed" (Decroux); b) *stillness*—one person remains immobile in the midst of a meandering crowd; c) *rhythm*—the beat or the breath that breaks the accepted pacing of the action; d) *intensity*—in some of Grotowski's work, the intensity was so great at certain moments that the audience sat watching, eyes rivetted, hardly daring to breathe; e) *contrast* or *contradiction*—Brecht used contradiction to bring a moment closer and make it clearer, often through music; Beckett was fond of contrasting emotions.

During the work, certain ideas and moments will be grabbed, pushed forward, or gently eased into place. Others will be held back, restrained. Still others will be used for one fleeting moment or perhaps they will be unceasingly repeated. There will be moments of explosion and others of stillness. By distancing thoughts and emotions, we can emphasize them, much as if we were in the inside of a lighthouse safe from the storm—for the moment—but the danger is never far away.

Costumes, mask, color, language, music, gesture—all must not be allowed to serve as crutches. They must be seen as visual and sonorous parts of the whole. They are theatrical aids, the result of discovery during the rehearsal process. They are to be used with awareness and choice.

In the 1960s there was a production of *La Vie Parisienne* in Paris, (Odeon-Barrault). Downstage, a gay, fast, colorful, energetic scene was taking place. But gradually the audience became aware of a solitary, tall, dark figure, moving almost imperceptibly across the rear of the stage, his back to the audience. By the end of the scene, the entire focus of the audience was on this slow, intense figure, so distanced from the rest of the action. In this way, Barrault focused his audience, making it watch and think.

A movement does not simply replace words, nor are words ever merely decorative. Words beautiful and the voice beautiful are distracting, much in the way that superfluous (though perhaps beautiful) movement in the space is meaningless.

Often, the use of nonrealistic, nonliterary images can be used to communicate a thought with great clarity and theatrical authority. This does not imply exaggerated images, but rather the conscious emphasizing of some things over others.

Conclusion

Every program of training for the actor and director must include exercises in the creating of theatre, along with the study of the skills necessary for a creative rehearsal process. Creating theatre is a collective work, requiring generosity at every level, among its many participants. There is a lot to be said for actors and directors working closely together, sharing one another's tasks and exchanging their roles.

Theatre can instill in the audience feelings and ideas that will remain with them long after the event. It is the theatre's creators who offer the audience this possibility.

5 | The Actor and Other Performance Skills

PHYSICAL TRAINING for the actor has long been concerned with what is perceived to be an actor's physical needs. How wonderful, it's been thought, if actors were in control of their bodies much as dancers are and able to move with the same facility! As a result, dance techniques of various sorts have often provided the basis for an actor's physical training. In much the same way, it's been recognized that many texts, especially classical ones, demand fencing and stage fighting. So these skills, as well, have traditionally been incorporated into the actor's curriculum. In my day, men were taken off to fencing classes, while the women were taught to faint! Movement programs have often reflected and complemented the general thrust or ideology of the institution or drama school of which they are a part, and often, out of necessity, a program has emphasized the strengths of the available movement teachers. And so, in a haphazard fashion, actors have been offered their "physical training." No one argues that actors need movement or "body" work; but there has been far too little serious thought about what is being offered as physical training, and why.

This chapter takes a look at certain of the physical performance arts and their relationship to the actor. We must consider at which point, if at all, the skill in itself (or the technique leading to that particular skill) is relevant to the actor's training. If not, is it perhaps in contradiction to such training? In order to do this, it is necessary to look, as well, at the training needed to obtain a "performance level" in these various skills being discussed.

What is not in discussion here is whether or not an actor should be able to tap, juggle, fire-eat, swing from a trapeze, or tumble—all very well. Obviously, the more performance skills, the better. What is in question is whether or not such skills should be introduced in an actor's foundation training and under what criteria or expectations.

In earlier chapters I have introduced the idea of an actor's physical training (stage movement for actors) not as a series of skills, but rather as a skill in itself. We are looking for a process to prepare the actor to take on the demands of the performance space.

Ideally, this foundation training should result in the actor being prepared and ready to take on new demands and further skills in other performance arts. The actor should now be able to approach these new forms of intense training with a physicality and methodology that will serve him well. Any kind of mastery of dance, or acrobatics, or mime, for example, requires a demanding and specific training. Physical skills involve muscle memory and this implies a concentrated time commitment. Each movement-based performance art makes its own demands on strength and has its own processes, its own way of thinking about and developing a body. These specific demands cannot be served in a system that provides bits and pieces of such work, over a period of a couple of years, even allowing for a certain amount of regularity. To imply that any level of mastery will be achieved like this seems grossly dishonest. Nor do I find any kind of "lesser" training (the same technical skills made easier for the actor) acceptable, based on the assumption that this is all the actor will need. It is not good enough to be a good actor with a quasi physical vocabulary, any more than is it good enough for an actor to be a marvelous acrobat, or have wonderful command of illusionary mime techniques if the skills of the acting craft do not provide a firm basis for his performance work. Certainly, in a period when we are speaking more and more in terms of "combined arts," theatre needs performers skilled enough to create stimulating, exciting work.

What is possible is a physically well-trained actor who, when presenting himself to a mime or circus school, is able to take on and make use of these new skills with a greater facility as a direct result of his physical readiness. His understanding of the physical process will allow him to incorporate better these skills into his own work. But the specific training involved to achieve a performance level in these skills cannot be sidestepped, nor the time needed to do the training properly be eschewed. Often, a long, hard study is involved.

Movement for the actor is simply a different training, addressing different physical needs and skills than those of the dancer, acrobat, circus performer, or mime. An actor's training program must reflect this. Elements of all these skills may be adapted and incorporated into the work but in an actor's vocabulary, aimed at fulfilling an actor's needs. There isn't much of an argument over what is a good physical actor. What one wants to do is to demystify the phenomenon and to record what is involved in bringing together such an actor. If we are not talking about teaching an actor dance or acrobatics or martial arts, per se, during the period of foundation training, it is very important to see which work and exercises will best serve this period.

The confusion seems to lie in the questions of where and why certain methods are useful. It is most important never to forget that an actor is a performer, and that all movement work must relate to performance. This may not be equally true in other parts of an actor's training. Body work, and especially the use of relaxation, serves a very different purpose in voice work. This difference must not be ignored. Certain physical training programs which have been developed (some very recently) are far more relevant to voice training than to stage movement. They are not in contra-diction; simply they are serving different needs in the process of developing the whole actor.

At some point it will be necessary to take a long close look at nonperformance oriented movement training, as their goals and objectives may be in direct contradiction to the actor's needs (i.e., certain ideas of "fitness" or deep "relaxation,".

Too much concerning movement training for actors has been left to chance, dependent on the interests of the teachers or the drama schools. Often movement has not been an integral part of an actor's training simply because the process has not been thought through. This results in a hodgepodge of skills on offer, or, alternatively, the young actor finds himself workshop "hopping" in search of a bit of skill here and a bit of skill there. The young actor is left to make sense of, for example, a series of traveling movements through space in a dance class, relaxation exercises which leave him floating in another class and then standing immobile, with "secret relaxation," grounded, ready to act, in a mime class. Where and how do they all link up?

Obviously, the more one does with the body, the better, as long as one does not lose sight of the relationship of this work to the actor's needs. If an actor insists on weight training, or dance, he must be clear how this training will affect the body in the theatre space, and must be in control of this extraneous work. Physical work for the actor must be within the concept of a program, and integrated into the process of an actor's development. One must be very clear and honest concerning the necessary commitment of time towards achieving these goals. What can and cannot be accomplished within time restrictions? The dancer, the trapeze artist, the violinist—all understand the need to practice, to train; the work involved in acquiring skill. The actor, however, has often been encouraged to develop his charisma, his attractiveness, etc., and that, along with fitness, is all that has been physically expected of him. Stage presence and use of the space are acquired skills. We are looking for actors who find in their physicality a useful instrument.

At different levels and stages of training there will be different methods and demands. What needs clarifying are the goals. Only then will the methods also become clear. I think we may find that a great deal of the physical training traditionally offered to the actor is not only irrelevant to the actor, but condescending to the other performance skills. And at times it is downright detrimental.

The Actor and Mime

The qualities and skills that help to define the clear and articulate actor are, I find, the very same ones that make a clear, articulate mime. Mime, like commedia dell'arte and other forms of physically expressive theatre, is based on all the same rules of good acting craft. This is why, perhaps, they should be considered separately from other performance skills such as dance and circus. A mime's language is an actor's language, his craft the same as any other actor. There have been periods in theatre history when it has been assumed that an actor was just that, a mime.

The mime is foremost an actor, not a dancer or acrobat. Mime, at its best (as can be seen in the work of Chaplin, Keaton, Grock, Barrault, Marceau, and Popov) is the work of actors. However, it is exactly this element that is lacking in the work of many mimes and mime theatres today. We have, instead, exponents of technique or visual design, but they are not articulate actors. Their bodies seem to die in the stage space, behind their elaborate masks or clever movements. There is no drama, no humor, only emptiness.

It is precisely for these reasons that mime work and an actor's work are never in contradiction. This cannot necessarily be said for much dance, circus, and relaxation work.

Mime theatre is a form that requires a heightened skill of corporeal expression and therefore requires a specific training going beyond that of most actors. Mime training need not, though, be considered something separate, but rather an extension of an actor's training. A mime is a specialized actor whose work will necessarily be built on his understanding of the craft as a whole. It is the actor's craft that will make the articulate mime.

At the same time, mime, in itself, is a very precise, demanding theatre form and will most likely not be readily accessible within a general acting program. The same may necessarily be true of Grotowski and commedia work. However, many of the techniques in these theatre forms are very relevant to an actor's training and should permeate everywhere within the program. The foundation or basis for the clear visual actor can also be found to be an intrinsic part of mime technique. It, too, is concerned with a clear physical presence in the space. "Etre, c'est peser," said Decroux. Mime, like acting, is about what I call "taking the space." To have weight does not mean to be heavy or light, but rather to be present. It is a theatre of movement, yes, but a theatre of movement where every move must have a dramatic reason—it must be motivated. Mime theatre is based on physical interaction; people relate, converse. It is a theatre of dramatic movement.

**THE ESSENCE OF MIME IS BASED ON FINDING
THE ESSENCE OF NATURAL MOVEMENT**

It is here where mime is perhaps most in opposition to much dance Decroux's study of movement reflects this essence. He studied, as have all mimes, natural movement, ordinary, everyday occurrences. He was in search of the intrinsic nature of his subject; analysing a movement, he stripped it down and, in arriving at its essence, found the "poetry" of the moment. What is very special about Decroux's work was that he struggled to find a methodology, a language, to allow the actor to achieve, through movement, this moment. He depersonalized it, searching for an actor's technique.

He was concerned with putting what he referred to as "the emotional or dramatic event" into movement. *However, the movement comes out of the event. It is not merely imposed upon it* in an effort to find a way to express what one is after. No, the movement simply serves as a visual rendering. This is where I believe many actors, be they mimes or not, get blocked (and why this work is so relevant to all actors). "An idea must materialize itself. It is then material for theatre" (Decroux). Mime must give spirit to material things and carry reality to its ends—it is not enough "to represent work, but the spirit of the person doing it" (Decroux). In Decroux's study there seems to me to be so much which is relevant to all actors of all theatre. All too often, however, mimes, in their hurry to exploit that which appears to separate them from other actors (their mime techniques, their bags of tricks) forget that which is basic to their work. For Decroux, mime was to theatre as poetry is to literature—a means to get to the very essence of a human moment.

**THE MIME/ACTOR'S STUDY IS FOUNDED ON THE SAME
CONCERNS AS THOSE OF THE "SPEAKING ACTOR"**

In their training, actors and mime/actors share much of the same process. The approach to the work will necessarily be similar, as they are striving for the same goals and objectives—that of dramatic clarity. They will both need to analyze physicality and to understand what happens to the body under specific conditions and situations. What happens to the body, for example, after years of a certain type of work or as a result of aging? What happens, physically, when one sobs or laughs, and do they really differ? What happens to a body in the face of fear? It will want to retreat. It may do this by looking and running, but perhaps it will retreat by simply casting the eyes to the ground. Why do different bodies react so differently under different situations to the same emotion? What do we mean about levels of tension? What are the substantive physical differences between exhaustion caused by a hard fast race or by sustained hard work over many years? What causes bodies to physically manifest themselves in so many differing ways?

All actors and mime/actors must return to the basic questions of intentions and motivation. To be credible, the physical response must have a cause, be motivated. The mime/actor will take this physicalization of the impulse to its ultimate conclusion. For example, an actor may watch with interest something on the ground. The mime/actor will watch with the same interest, but rather than just look he will follow the physical impulse to its conclusion; that is, he will draw a line, physically, in space, from the point of sighting to the object of interest itself. An actor will hear a noise behind him and turn his head. The mime/actor will continue this movement to its end—a full turn.

Both sorts of actor will often find the essence of their character through the walk. So many sociological, historical, emotional, or physical qualities are reflected in the walk? What does the actor understand by the feel of the character's walk? What does the public understand when watching it?

Mime has often been concerned with ritualizing the ordinary—sleeping, eating, working, seducing. It is through the activities of everyday life that mime has attempted to clarify and arrive at the essential of human behavior. Sometimes mime has used comedy; at other times it has used highly abstract forms.

Though all actors will need their physical skills for the work of making the invisible visible, the mime/actor's theatre form will require an execution of movement skills beyond that of most actors. They will need to call on a different level of strength, of control, perhaps of flexibility. However, without the basic skill of listening and responding, and allowing the body to physically manifest the thought or emotion (with awareness always of where the movement begins—the "tugboat" of the movement), the work of any actor is meaningless.

Much theatre today functions without physically articulate actors by managing to hide them. Decroux spoke of the ultimate of this phenomenon when he spoke of a performance of "To be or not to be" performed behind a screen! Lights, costumes, props, sets, all help obscure that which is basic to theatre, the actor!

Such ideas mark a clear progression from the work of the Vieux-Colombier and have been reflected in much of the post-World War II European theatre. This is not only true in mime, but in other theatre forms as well, which now tend to be classified as "visual" theatre.

MIME LANGUAGE MUST BE LEARNED

"All the great poets who move us express pain...not with one's stomach, but in a learned language"(Decroux). Mime is no different.

The study of mime can lead to a long, detailed process. Often mime has not developed as a theatre form due to the mime/actor's desire for quickness—there has been a reluctance to take the time to study the form. In the rush to get into the stage space, the actor has found himself with a few techniques, but no language to adhere to. There are the clear exceptions. There are the companies or actors who use their language in an articulate manner, keeping in mind that theatre starts with a need to communicate. There is no mystery. Much of mime today is again finding its place within "ordinary theatre," and I find this a very comfortable place for it to be. It marks an understandable progression, or regression, for it has often been a part of many theatre forms.

What Decroux did was to develop a methodology towards these goals. "What I have done is to consider the human body as a keyboard of a piano. One key isolated from another" (Decroux).[1] He has defined this form of dramatic expression that doesn't replace words, but in which, like music and sculpture, there is no need for words.

It is a study of weight: of the image created through the transfer of weight and the moments between that transfer. Watch statues,

Decroux used to say. Notice the dignity of the weight forward or the foolishness of the weight back. Watch how people walk. Notice how weight held back produces the comic.

It is the study of the push and the pull as a means to understand work movement. For Decroux, mime movement was representational of work. It often seemed to me that his main concern for the study of work movement was an aesthetic one; others of us have been more interested in work movement in its sociological or historical connotations. Lecoq sees the push and pull beyond work, as the basis with which to understand much of human interaction. But for whatever purpose the push-pull will serve the theatre space, its study is there to be mastered before it can be used.

It is the study of intensity, rhythm, and design. It is the study of the relationship of movement to stillness. "How long to rest is the question of art"(Decroux). Or, as Decroux would quote from Chaplin, "Mime is immobility." Decroux defined farce as fast; drama as slower; tragedy as still more immobility. The relationship of the length of distance and time played an important role in this investigation.

The study is one of natural movement taken from its immediate, visible reality to its essential. In real life we are hindered by social mores (e.g., politeness) or real obstacles (e.g., walls) from showing that which we wish. In mime, through essence, freed from reality, we may take an action or an emotion and bring it to its conclusion.

"In representing a thing you must represent its spirit and its reality. You can't just show the thing itself" (Decroux). Here, in this statement, we find and understand why mime can be a unique and valuable theatre form. However, much of mime in the past decade has not been concerned with these qualities. Why this is true is another discussion probably related to the state of theatre as a whole: the fumbling of its writers, the basis of its financing, of the confusion surrounding its search for a new aesthetic.

With a grand contempt for all that is mediocre, this anti-social socialist often found himself isolated. But it is perhaps this single-minded determination that has allowed him to create almost single-handedly a process, a technique, a common language for mime. He has provided mimes the basis with which they may express themselves as corporeal actors, able to move from style to style with artistic freedom and responsibility. What Decroux has done is to provide what Marcel Marceau has called "a grammar." Decroux was primarily a teacher of actors; his technique is as valid for what he calls "speaking actors" as it is for mime actors. I do not find his ideas and techniques limited to his theatre or philosophy. Though, at times, he has seemed enamoured with the form, to the detriment of content (his concept of "l'homme d'ile" is a good example of this), it is exactly his language that frees an actor to be physically clear in saying what he wishes, how he wishes. The more I teach actors, the more I find I come back to his ideas when, for example, I need to unstick a stuck actor. These ideas are formulated in a very clear understanding of an actor's craft. The work is extremely concrete, concerned with a study of people and movement. It is uncluttered: it is not abstract, it is essential. It is a means to assure an actor of corporeal awareness and control. Always working from the interior, Decroux insists on techniques (inner monologue, breath, concept of the "motor of a movement," etc.) that allow the actor to bring the interior to the corporeal surface. This liberates actors much in the way clear diction does. The method is not a style, nor is it, in itself, theatre. It is simply an actor's physical language. It is the ability to give and receive, to interact and communicate, through a glance, a breath, a sigh, an explosion.

The following is the text from a mime piece by "The Mime Project," a San Francisco-based mime company of the mid-'70s, entitled "Hommage à Decroux." The words are based on our notes from Decroux's classes in the early '60s, early '70s.

Hommage à Decroux

1. Mime is immobility...

2. Living immobility; it breathes.

3. When man was born, he arose and looked about and found the stars, the moon, the ocean, the trees, but he never saw when they began.

4. To be is to have weight.

5. Knowing when to act is the question of art.

6. Body movement is a violin, a piano, and sometimes a cloud.

7. Everything is beautiful as long as you do it on purpose.

8. A man and a woman. They are seated on a beach at the turn of the century. They are shaded by an old-fashioned canopy. She is sewing peacefully. He is close by watching her. Suddenly, with no sign of wind, the canopy rises and slowly falls. His eyes catch hers. "Je vous aime, Madame."

9. Mime is a representation of work.

10. Work is the measure of man. Man is the measure of dance.

11. A dancer is a bird, flapping his wings, striving to reach the heavens. A mime is the bird sweeping down to Earth.

12. One must find the just distance.

13. A horse is more beautiful held by reins. Drama is conflict.

14. Drama is always being on a precipice.

15. Security is "bourgeois."

16. No one knows when the thief will come.

17. He judged himself because he was surprised.

18. Most men try to make life rhythmical, concise, to get things to depart and arrive on time. Artists try to put accident into this rhythm.

19. Rhythm in movement equals verse in poetry.

20. Poetry troubles. Things reassure.

21. The enemies of art are utility, laziness, and fear.

22. It is easier to go away from truth.

23. A mime is both subject and object; like a surgeon who opens his stomach.

24. Man cannot see what he is able to touch, nor touch what he sees ...at the moment of embrace.

25. A polite man is altruistic; he would never stab the eyes of space.

26. He is straight. Reason is straight. Passion is round. It is with squares you make circles.

27. Classicism exists in not showing everything. Everything in little; little in everything.

28. Meditation, thought, hesitation, petrification, doubt....

29. There is nothing new under the sun....

30. Beauty breaths. Black in painting, holes in sculpture, silence in music, and rest in mime.

31. Rest is a gentle thing, like the fall of night.

The words are out of context. They belong to a piece of visual theatre. They are the words selected by a group of people in a specific period of time. But perhaps today they offer a basis for theatre workers to discard, or adopt and expand.

AS A THEATRE FORM AND ACTOR'S TECHNIQUE, MIME IS OF GREAT RELEVANCE TO AN ACTOR'S CRAFT

An actor's, and a mime/actor's task is the same. However, to be able to express oneself corporeally in a dramatic form, with no need for words, requires a physical training beyond that which is incorporated into most theatre studies. It is a study in itself. Mastering the physical skills necessary to express oneself as a mime is a long process. The principles, however, involved in the work, are universal to all actor's needs. Such a method of work makes the process towards the essential, towards the credible, both more efficient and more attainable.

The Actor and commedia dell'arte

A specific mention of commedia must be made in order to emphasize its important place in a contemporary actor's vocabulary. One must emphasize, as well, its unique characteristics and skills which require of the commedia actor a specific study and commitment.

Many commedia techniques offer the actor important aids in bringing into the stage space both his ideas and characters. Learning how to develop and control the large, essential, archetypical characters of commedia is the logical progression from the character work already done in foundation acting. The step from a three-dimensional "realistic" character, to a three-dimensional archetype, is not readily obvious, nor an easy one. The link, however, is a very important one if nonnaturalistic acting is not to become cardboard acting. This is true, whether we are talking about clowning, mime, epic theatre or a Dario Fo play. Commedia offers a wonderful process in which to free actors from the limitations of television acting. A study of the lazzi and other commedia techniques is very much a part of an actor's work, both for comic timing and character interactions. It provides an especially rich material for developing an actor's imagination.

However, it must not be assumed that knowing about commedia is the same as doing it well. It is a very specialized form, requiring a mastery of skills in tumbling, mask work, comic timing, improvisation, etc. Like mime, nothing is more boring or irrelevant than mediocre commedia, especially when used in a modern context.

Commedia is one of the specialist skills I would most encourage actors to pursue and which will serve today's actor very well indeed. Lecoq has called it an excellent point of reference for the actor to understand the use of physicality. If I mention it here, only briefly, it is because there is much written on the subject to which an actor may refer. Commedia offers actors a veritable plethora of theatrical experience and skills.

There are many other forms of physical theatre that provide exciting vehicles for an actor's development, e.g., Peking Opera, various Japanese and other eastern theatre forms, traditional clowning techniques, as well as ideas and methods developed by people like Meyerhold and Grotowski. When an actor brings a well-trained actor's body to the study of these forms and techniques, they can become a vital and relevant part of his development and available to him with greater facility and alacrity.

The Actor and Circus/Acrobatic Skills

CIRCUS AND THE PHYSICAL ACTOR - WHAT ROLE DOES CIRCUS AND DO CIRCUS TECHNIQUES PLAY IN THE "ORDINARY" ACTOR'S CRAFT?

Both traditional circus and "new" circus are currently in the process of defining and redefining what circus is all about. What does circus entail? What does it serve, to whom and why? Circus is today both going into and emerging from a large range of communities. Certain circuses have taken the traditional skills to new heights of enchantment (I think here of the Chinese). Others have taken these skills to create performances bordering on theatre. Wherein is the magic of circus? What are the skills specific to circus and under what circumstances does and should circus thrive?

There are many skills that circus has traditionally incorporated into performance: juggling, uni- and bicycle tricks, tumbling, trapeze, rope walking, etc.. While they may not all be death-defying, they have enthralled the public exactly because they represent something unusual, something often very difficult. They are exciting *because* they are out of the ordinary. Many of these skills are accessible with practice and time, but it cannot be forgotten that it is the level and sheer beauty of skill, presented with visual excitement (often with elements of surprise—the basis of comedy) that has fascinated so many for so long. (The more balls a juggler is working with; the more people on the bicycle; the more extraordinary the trick on the tightrope). When well-presented, circus is a glorious celebration of skill—it delights, it surprises, it shocks, it inspires.

There are many circuses today whose work is very close to that of theatre. Into their circus language they have integrated clear thoughts and are concerned with communicating ideas through statements and interactions. But their language remains that of circus techniques, and the more highly skilled they are, the clearer and more successful they are. There are some small circuses (in Catalonia, for example), that combine a very fine example of circus craft with acting and theatre craft. However, there are also many circuses in which, it would seem, high energy, enthusiasm and good intentions have been substituted for the high skill that constitutes the essence of circus.

As for the actor who would incorporate circus skills into his work, it must be understood that it takes a great deal of training and practice to bring many circus skills to a performance level, in a circus/theatre context. Certainly a basis for some of the work can be learned in a workshop, but a tremendous commitment of time on the part of the actor is necessary to reach the point where these skills can be made use of in the performance space.

ACROBATICS AND TUMBLING AS ACTOR'S SKILLS

When speaking about tumbling and acrobatics as an actor's skill, we must indicate immediately that what a circus acrobat does on a trampoline or trapeze involves a different language from that of the actor. This is not to say that an actor couldn't make fine use of these skills, but acrobatic expertise is only as useful as is the actor's ability to incorporate it into the needs of the theatre moment. An actor may dive through the space, but this must not be done as an acrobat, but rather as a character who is doing such a thing for a well-motivated reason! It is not important from what height a fall takes place. It is important, rather, that the context in which the fall happens is clear. Ideally, the audience will never identify the fall with acrobatic skill. It is wonderful when actors have such skills and incorporate them well. Here we cannot help but think of Buster Keaton or Ekkehard Schall. However, a roll, a dive, or a flip existing for no reason other than to show off a skill is worse than useless; it distracts from the dramatic moment. The focus changes and the carefully created continuity and rhythm are lost. Tumbling and acrobatic skills must simply be *extensions* of an actor's language. By this, we mean the ability of the actor to take a natural movement and to extend it to the ultimate. Now, that is useful!

Such skills are integral to much stylized theatre work: Commedia, stage fighting, Peking Opera, knock-about-comedy, etc. But one must never lose sight of the word *integral*. The movement is part of the dramatic moment; it is the result of something that has happened and in itself will cause the continuation of the action. Acrobatic skill simply permits the actor to take a natural response to its physical limit.

When incorporated into the framework of the initial physical training, the confidence tumbling can give actors is invaluable. How to roll, how to fall, how to avoid injury, awareness of all the parts of the body (even when upside down or in mid-air) is all very basic to an actor's needs. At the same time, the actor is learning to listen to and follow inner rhythm and be able to respond and develop the rhythm of the scene, under any circumstance.

As the requirements of physical expression are expanded, and as the actor is more able to depend on his body, acrobatic skills for the actor should be insisted upon both in the classroom space and in rehearsal situations. The actor must search for the best way to incorporate the daily physical skill work into the performance space. The two should never be far apart. The step by step process of taking the work out of the classroom and into the theatre is extremely important. The control, the awareness, the strength, the spring, the physical confidence found in the classroom, must not be lost. It is a question of absorbing this language into the actor's imagination. Often, it is at this point that a movement director can be very helpful; as a third eye the movement director will search for the best solution to achieve visually that which one is after. But the responsibility lies in the body of the actor. If he is to use acrobatics as his means of expression, the skills must be at his fingertips.

I cannot emphasize enough the need for careful, clear teaching, especially at the moment when the actor begins to acquire the skills as his own. It is an intense training to be able to achieve the skill level of a tumbling actor. It is a training that will differ from that of the circus performer. Acrobatic skills are simply serving a very different purpose.

STAGE-FIGHTING—A THEATRE SKILL OF ILLUSION

Stage-fighting, hand to hand or with weapons, is a practical response to demands of the theatre. As the actor takes on board this work, he must be clear as to why the fight is happening (dramatic purpose) and what the audience is seeing (illusion).

To acquire stage-fighting skills, the actor will need a coordinated, aware body. The work is truly ensemble work involving very close physical contact with the other actors. The actors are interdependent and must have trust in each other's skills. They depend on each other to be in the right spot at the right moment, in the right position and at the right degree of readiness, both physically and mentally. The task is specific. As James Hennessy, British stage-fight teacher and actor, puts it: "responsibility for self; responsibility to each other; responsibility to character." Stage fighting is the physicalization of conflict in theatre and therefore involves the craft of acting as well as the movement skills of acrobatics, tumbling, and mime. Along with these skills is the need for constant analysis of history and style—how people fought, when and why, etc.

Stage fighting is not weapon fighting as a sport, nor is it a martial art. The teacher must understand this difference. Making a fight look believable, with no one getting hurt, is the task. An obvious progression from basic physical training of the actor and acrobatics, it is a skill requiring time and practice. If the well-trained body takes on this craft, perfecting the tricks of the trade, it is an extremely useful tool for the actor. The role of the third-eye, as in all illusion work, is invaluable.

The Actor and Dance

Dance-based movement has long been a part of an actor's training. Actors have been exposed to contemporary dance, new dance, ballet barre, floor barre, period dance, tap, jazz, etc., depending, at best, on the training program's general thrust, or, at worst, on an unthought-out belief that it would be a good thing if actors could move like dancers. Without posing the questions of *why* this should necessarily be true, or *how* this should be achieved under the specific conditions of an actor's training, a variety of dance techniques find themselves a part of acting programs. If there is not clear thought about how such work is or is not integral to the rest of the work, such an approach must necessarily be full of intrinsic dangers.

The questions of *when*, and indeed, *if* dance is to be introduced into such programs must be answered after we look at why dance is taught in the first place. What can dance techniques achieve for actors? Without answers to such questions, we fall into a great many contradictions and frustrations. " A quoi se sert?" Decroux would demand!

DANCE: IS IT A USEFUL TOOL FOR DEVELOPING THE PHYSICALLY ARTICULATE ACTOR?

Obviously, the more movement work to be incorporated into an actor's training from the beginning the better. The question here is what are the best methods to achieve the physical language of the actor?

In the first place, we are looking for a technique that will develop *alignment*—the correct placement of the head on neck, on waist, on pelvis, etc. This requires a strong back, and an acute personal awareness of one's body; whether in stillness or in the midst of physical exercise or in simple everyday movement such as sitting or walking. In other words, we need a technique that is based on precision and detail, on awareness of breath, and the use and placement of weight.

Then we are looking for techniques that will develop strength, flexibility, coordination and awareness—elements that will permit the actor to use the body with confidence: the confidence to know that the feet, legs, back, etc. will indeed hold him up and permit him to react physically! The actor's body must be able to sustain that which has been achieved, no matter what the physical or emotional demands.

We need, as well, a technique that will demand a *minimum of effort* to achieve the movement we are after. Unlike the athlete or dancer, who often are literally striving for "greater heights," the actor will need to leap up perhaps once in an evening. That leap, however, will always be in response to a stimulus. The actor may find himself running down the stairs, in full conversation, sustaining all the while his dramatic impulse. In doing this, the actor must know how much effort it will take to achieve the action and use no more. "Don't work so hard" one often hears a director telling the actor. What the director is saying is don't strain, don't use excess strength. The actor must find the minimum strength needed.

An actor's movement methodology must be based on a *minimum of movement*. It must be a technique concerned with movement economy, in which each movement exists for a dramatic reason, and where clarity is achieved through the lack of all excess and the power of stillness.

Most of all, we are looking for a technique that will always be aware of the *cause of a movement*. Most movement finds its source in the interior. Through breath (emotion) or decision (thought), it manifests itself physically, out through the body and limbs. Never does the actor, for example, rise up on tiptoe by lifting his heels and simply putting himself into such a position. Rather, something has caused him to rise up; the movement is a response to an internal cause (such as an uplifting idea) or an external cause (such as a sudden gust of wind). Action is motivated; the actor needs to move. If an actor crosses the space, be it by walking or running, by a skip or a dive, there must be a reason to do so. Inner rhythm is the key here. One must listen to one's own music; the interior music to which the action responds.

Obviously, certain dance techniques may fulfill certain of these needs. At the same time, much of dance work is in distinct opposition. An actor's basic actions are to stand and walk. There is a feeling of being grounded—a sense of simultaneously pulling up and pushing into the ground. Yet the act of walking is one of the most difficult things for a dancer to do. Why? I think the answer can be found if one looks into the objectives of dance training. What is the dancer trying to achieve or express in the performance space? How does this differ from other physical performance forms?

If certain dance techniques are to be used as a part of an actor's training, they must be incorporated into the specific requirements of the actor. Dance teachers, teaching actors, must be acutely aware of this and attentive in analyzing the differences between a dancer's and an actor's needs. A ballet barre taught by an actor/dancer can be very different from the same being taught by a dancer. Many dance teachers are aware of these contradictions and are addressing the work with their own methodology. However, dance for the non-dancer is a field to be further investigated. In many ways, much of the new dance work for actors, finds itself addressing the needs of voice work perhaps more than actor's movement. Recreational dance, again, is in almost direct contradiction to the actor's use of dance as an element of performance.

Often dance teachers find themselves separated from the rest of the actors' training program. They have been brought in for their expertise, to teach dance once or twice a week for an agreed period of time. Both teachers and students become frustrated by the slowness of progress, and the lack of any coherence in the work. The absence of an understanding of the needs of dance movement is most clearly reflected by the timetabling. Days and days go by, when the process is outright stopped. One class per week gets no one anywhere. But the system keeps on, held by the belief that a class most weeks over a couple of years will result in something. Dancers know better. Dance is an intense training, demanding constant, often repetitive work, with a clear progression in skill demands. In such a situation all that is feasible for the dance teacher to do is to lower the demands and expectations and hope the exercises will have some effect. This is exactly what happens.

Dance language is a different language from an actor's language. Moving to music or an external beat is a different skill from movement that is a direct reflection of an inner rhythm. Dancers listen to the beat or tempo; actors listen to their breath. An actor dances in response to a dramatic situation. Actors will always need to sing their music, because they are following an impulse—an urge to dance. They never count the beat. In this way, they sustain their dramatic intention. The character's inner rhythms interact with the rhythm of the music, and it is this that determines how the character dances. The actor must make dramatic sense of his movement. The character will not only be relating to the dance steps, but also to the dramatic context in which the dancing is taking place. The actor must be able to execute intricate and strenuous movement while sustaining his character's objectives. He will be using the minimum of energy necessary to execute the movement. Correct breathing and relaxation are of utmost importance.

There is a widely held belief that dancers "don't breath," or that they do "reverse breathing." Why this should be intrinsically true to dance movement is unclear. I see no reason why one can't do a series of leaps or a ballet barre and not only breathe properly but speak as well. Many dance and voice teachers have turned their direction to this apparent contradiction and are working it out.

Like many physical methods of training, dance training has often been full of a variety of mannered uses of the body. But dancers aren't married to these mannerisms. At the same time, there is no reason why an actor should move "like a dancer" just because he is dancing!

These are questions, however, that dancers must take great care about when dealing with actors. Actors will need to move and speak at the same time and make sense of both. If dancers tend to repeat movement and to enjoy a movement for its design and feel in the space (for its aesthetic value), often evoking a sense of ease and lightness, an actor's use of movement will necessarily be very different. An actor's movement will never exist in and for itself but will be motivated by the dramatic moment. The actor will take the space with weight, presence, and often stillness. An actor's movement must never be imposed or choreographed but rather must reflect or be in response to the moment. Only then can an action perhaps be decided upon. And like any other action of the actor, the motivation for it must be "refound" at each rehearsal or performance.

Dance in all its forms has discovered a great deal about physicality. Its analysis of body, of strength and flexibility, of coordination, of support and balance, of avoidance of injury, etc. are as relevant to the actor as they are to the dancer. The question is how this knowledge is presented to the actor and in what context. The use of turnout, for example, to free the actor to move quickly, to change direction, to help him balance, and to help avoid knee injury, etc. is invaluable, when presented in the context of an actor's needs. The search for harmony of movement is a search relevant to both a dancer and actor, but always in relation to their own language of communication. Certain parts of the dancer's rich vocabulary may be borrowed and incorporated into an actor's movement training. But this will necessarily be a very different thing from a dance class.

Decroux defined the differences between dance and mime. He could have been speaking about dance and acting:

> Dance is abstract and based on music. Mime is concrete and based on life. Dance flows like a stream. Mime moves with the natural plunge and lunge of the muscles. Dance is ecstatic and vertical. Mime earthy and horizontal. The dancer works with the leap; the mime with the walk.[2]

DANCE PERFORMANCE BY ACTORS

An actor must be prepared for the demands of dance that may be incorporated into an actor's performance. This could be anything from a minuet, to a tango; from disco dancing to a balletic lift. Perhaps it will be a question of simply stepping "in time" in order to enliven a song. Sometimes a whole scene will be conceived in dance-like movement. How do we get an actor to do all this? What is the best way to prepare an actor for such demands and under what expectations should such demands be made? I think it is grossly unfair and dishonest to let an actor believe that with a class or two a week in dance, over a period of a couple of years, he will be sufficiently skilled to think of himself as an actor/dancer. Dance is an extremely valuable skill for an actor to have. It is important to encourage those with previous training to maintain their skill level and, at the same time, encourage those who are keen to find the time to train intensely at some point, in order to make best use of this ability and interest.

The actor who has developed a responsive, coordinated, and controlled body should, I believe, be introduced to dance methodology and language in a intensive manner so that he can understand how such work may be of use in the performance space. (The well-trained physical actor, never having done period dance, as such, should now be able to learn and make use of such movement, with much more efficiency than if he has had snippets of it across a few terms, or a few bits and pieces in the odd workshop). Intensive study with a prepared body will provide both a method and approach that then can be applied to the performance situation. Usually there will be the guidance of the expert—the choreographer. We are not looking for the trained dancer, but rather the actor who can pick up steps quickly, respond to music physically, and move with others in a shared space without bumping and stepping on toes. A great deal depends on the director's or choreographer's ability to stage dance work for nondancers. This is a specific skill in itself.

We have implied that sparse dance classes at an early point in training can be in direct contradiction to the other work an actor may be doing. However, dance, introduced at a later stage, with performance goals in mind, is a great asset to any actor's work. He should now be able to grasp the dance methodology with an actor's skill. He will be able to make dramatic sense of movement to music. Working closely with others in the space takes on a new dimension. Several classes per week, at minimum, will permit an understanding of how dance movement works, and how, for example, it differs from other movement work. The actor will learn how to take on the work and proper work methods for dance. It is helpful if the work involves the sort of dance situations in which an actor might find himself: dancing waltzes, or tangos, or country dances; doing line work, lifts,and work involving close ensemble movement to music, for example. As the skill level develops, this work becomes more and more accessible. The actor is learning to present himself in a dance vocabulary, to be confident and clear in a musical number. These are the skills that should be on offer. It is a part of an actor's training that must be thought out and well conceived.

The Breath, Relaxation, Voice, and Movement Training

Stage movement, corporeal expression, movement for actors—all are attempts to describe the physical preparation that will enable the actor to be physically responsive in the performance space. They imply the need to train actors to be able to create visually clear, believable images and statements. Very early on, an actor's training will need to be concerned with space and with the interactions and relationships of those within that space. Often it is through watching others that the objectives of this work become clear in the actor's mind. The role of inner rhythm and its relationship to breath are perhaps best defined as the actor actually sees and analyses a responsive, alive actor at work. The actor begins to understand his task from the point of view of the audience,and the body as a physically expressive instrument takes on a meaning.

The goal is to prepare the body to move (respond) with visual clarity, as a result of and in the context of the dramatic moment. To achieve this, the body must be aware, aligned, in control, and breathing properly. But beyond these needs are the needs of the actor to develop with clarity the relationship of his body to the space and to the others in that space; always listening and responding, offering and receiving.

It is therefore necessary that actors learn from the very beginning to control and use energy. They must know how, for example, to sustain very high energy; without strain, without tension, never forgetting to use the minimum energy necessary to achieve the necessary dramatic moment. To do this one works with what is called a "secret relaxation." The actor must never be collapsed. He must always be ready to act. The neutral, relaxed actor is very present, firm in the space, aware of every muscle, in control, awake, alive. Grounded, with weight, he is ready. Taking energy up or down is a result of the dramatic moment, the result of the actor's objective. Relaxation, in these terms, is very conscious—the actor will constantly be "checking out" his body. There is, however, no reason why the actor, under such circumstances, shouldn't be breathing properly. "Reverse breathing," or holding one's breath, and all those ideas that are associated with dancers and "movers" in general are not implicit to demanding physical work. In fact, quite the contrary. Actors must be constantly aware of the need to control tensions, and of breathing properly, even when upside down. *Relaxation must be linked to the physical demands of an actor's work;* breath will take an actor to the action, and will dictate how an actor will move only when the body is at its maximum awareness and responsiveness.

In preparing the body for voice work, there well may be concerns and requirements that differ from those that we have been speaking about in context of the movement work. It is true that both are looking for alignment, for personal physical awareness, for control, and for proper breathing; both are thoroughly physical and concerned with the actor's instrument. But it is also possible that, especially during the beginning stages, voice work will necessarily have another emphasis and other goals. As the training of voice has taken on a more and more physical base in the past couple of decades, there has often been the assumption that the means of achieving the actor's physical skills are the same. Attempts are made to link up the voice and movement programs and to work in tandem. Some body and movement based work, such as Alexander Technique, Laban, and Feldenkrais have found a formidable place in voice training. Obviously, both voice and movement work are concerned with preparing and training the body. But if the emphasis and tasks are different, so, too, must be the approach. What appears to be most contentious is the question of the process and timing of an actor's development, i.e., what work is done and when. It must be recognized that the work is addressing, simultaneously, many aspects of an actor's training. They are not in contradiction, but neither are the immediate goals necessarily the same. At some point the work will all come together, and we shall have an actor capable of using his body as a complete entity, through sound and movement.

It is the responsibility of those working in these fields to take on board these differences. "Dancers don't breath"—so by all means avoid a ballet barre! No! Total relaxation is a good thing, therefore Feldenkrais work can be given as a warm-up, and never mind if actors can't find or feel their bodies for the rest of rehearsal. No! But it is possible to work hard and breathe properly, just as it is possible to regain centered muscular control after deep relaxation. It is necessary that these contradictions be addressed and catered for with the idea that we are all working for the physically explicit *actor*. Movement classes will be emphasizing the body as a means of expression, preparing the body for the total physical expression of the dramatic moment. Again, we must return and look at the elements of movement: *rhythm*—the listening to the body's music and its responses to inner rhythm, as reflected, through the breath, in the actor's physical expression; *intensity*—the creative use of tension: using the intensity of a movement to direct the audience's focus; and *design*—the image that a body or bodies create through their actions and what such an image communicates, e.g., a leg, bent or straight; a head, isolated or in relationship to someone else's head, etc.

Different bodies respond to different demands at different points in their development. It is very important that all tutors in voice, in movement, and in acting, be aware of the individual actor; his blocks, his progressions. The teaching must not confuse individual needs and the immediate apparent demands of the pedagogical program. Often, for example, the same tensions will manifest themselves in both the voice and movement work. But it is equally possible that this won't happen. It is necessary to develop all parts of an actor's physicality simultaneously. The process is continuous; but there will be different rates of progression and different immediate needs in the different areas of work. There must be a constant dialogue between tutors and actors. The ultimate goals must be clear to all and only then can what appear to be contradictions be successfully defined and the process of development be assured.

Conclusion

An actor's training must not treat the physical performance skills superficially. Not only can this be dangerous, leading to injury (acrobatics, stage fighting, etc.), but it can result in inarticulate theatre. Everywhere there are semi-skilled actors. They are full of energy, good will, tricks, and sometimes ideas. But they are physically "gagged." Skills are what free an actor to go further, to heighten a statement or to find the best way to present an idea clearly. (In a production of *Jesus Christ, Superstar*, for example, we wanted Judas to fall from high scaffolding into an abyss. This required a lot of skill from several actors, but it achieved the statement we were after.)

At the same time, skills must serve the whole. Even a theatrical interlude set within a performance will have a purpose and say something to an audience. Skills are not to be displayed: a dance number here, or an illusionary trick there; but rather they are there for the actor to use. It is hoped that the technique itself will go unobserved.

The skilled actor is simply that—a skilled *actor*. Additional skills will allow him to specialize, to take theatre further, through clowning, or mime or music, etc. The skilled actor's stage is enormous...from visually concrete theatre and characters to theatre like that of Yves Lebretan that is concerned with "the internal thought that impels" the characters....[3] But an actor's task remains the same. He is always an actor/mime, or an actor/clown, or an actor/acrobat. The process of teaching must reflect this. An actor must be given the tools of his trade; the understanding of methods. By this we mean an understanding of what he must do in order to obtain the skills of dance, or mime, or acrobatic movement. But this process must be taught in context of an actor's needs, which will be different from those of a dancer or acrobat. The study is that of the relationship of complex movement skills to the mundane, everyday movement of the actor, whose character sits, walks, stands, runs, goes up and down stairs, etc.

The definition of good or "interesting" theatre is constantly both changing and broadening. At the same time, there is often a tendency to dismiss or categorize. New demands are made on the actor and often theatre "styles" and theatrical techniques and tricks are offered as a way forward. But the actor will find them, in themselves, meaningless and empty. "Physical theatre," "visual theatre," "total theatre," etc., like any other theatre (and after all, all theatre is physical, visual, etc.), is about communication. No matter what the intent of the theatre work, this is the thought that must serve as the point of departure in its creation.

Epilogue
The Actor in the Eyes of the Beholder

THE EVENT THAT ULTIMATELY materializes in the theatre space is the creation of a team consisting of writers, actors, directors, designers, musicians, technicians, and others. Combining their imagination and intellect, this team has searched for the best way possible to present their thoughts and feelings theatrically. In the center of this creative process is the actor, who, by the very nature of his work, will guide and influence the audience. In his role as direct communicator to the public, the actor shoulders a very specific responsibility. Often it is the actor who serves as the catalyst for the entire team.

In the process of creation, his perspective of the work will be reflected along with that of the rest of the team. In no way can this be denied. His task is to bring alive and make visible the ideas encompassed in the work. With extreme sensitivity, he will take in and then respond to the material. He will analyze it, make decisions about his discoveries, and be instrumental in guiding the work into clear dramatic statements.

The actor's skills, i.e., observation, concentration, offering and receiving, analysis, objectives and the physical actions necessary to achieve these objectives, etc., are valid only if they result in clearly manifested images, created in the context of the dramatic moment. The actor's instrument is his body. This book has been concerned with how an actor can learn to use his instrument with imagination, skill and responsibility.

Depending on historical moments and cultural tendencies, the actor's physicality has been looked upon with delighted or jaundiced eyes. Often, under the dominating influences of film and television or in periods when theatre has been primarily escapist, we have seen the attractive body (culturally defined, of course), to be the principle concern of an actor's physical training. In the drama schools of the fifties and sixties, the "girls" were told to lose five pounds and the "boys"to lift weights. Fencing was taught for Shakespeare, while in contemporary dance classes "run, run,leaps" across the floor were taught to help identify a feeling of high energy and physical fun.

No one doubts the need for an actor to have a prepared body. However, the actor's specific physical needs have seldom been clearly defined. The question of how to articulate ideas and feelings visually in an imaginative, theatrical language has remained problematic. The need for the attractive body, full of energy and strength, is addressed; perhaps a smattering of physical performance skills are offered. The result has been the floundering, physically vague, indecisive actor, who seems to disappear the moment there are no words to hide behind.

Certainly there is a great heritage of movement theatre to serve as a basis for our study, as well as the work on the actor's physical training process from people like Meyerhold and Decroux. But all too often the actual teaching of an actor's physicality has been random and left to chance or centered around the teaching of a movement "guru."

The actor's physical training is a skill in itself, and not to be confused with other movement skills. A virtuoso of physical skills is not necessarily a good physical actor. An actor's training must be freeing and provide the basis from which the body, as an actor's instrument, can be used to best express the dramatic moment.

The actor's movement work must not be taught solely in the isolation of a classroom, far removed from the performance space. Acting skills and an actor's movement skills are inseparable. This doesn't mean that classes can't be separated, but the links to improvisation work, to text analysis, to character work, and to the rehearsal process must be clearly defined and eventually they must all come together. The actor has specific physical needs that must be addressed if he is to make sense and use of such acting techniques as the "physical action" or the "physical gestus", or "complicité".

"Physicality informs"..."We first see a body" (Decroux). Everything an actor does in the stage space is seen and is interpreted by the audience. What he does is what he is in the eyes of the beholder.

An actor's training must be concerned not only with freeing an actor's physical imagination, but with developing it as well. A finely-tuned awareness of the possibilities of the creative instrument along with the physical control of this instrument are the prerequisites for any physically articulate actor. An actor can't just hope that something will happen; he must make it happen. He must follow the impulses originating from the inner rhythm. He must be sensitive to breath, a gasp, a sigh perhaps, and to the most subtle of muscular reactions. A vibrant, alive presence isn't obtained by just doing things, but rather by identifying and developing physical feelings. In this way the actor can avoid the cliché and generality, and be able to find the essence of the dramatic moment with credibility and clarity.

We have tried to study and define the actor's task, to look at the "metier". There are differing methods that will address the differing cultural and historical needs of the actor. But the sense of physical process, and the time and manner given to this process, cannot be ignored.

Theatre is not "a finely-written play to be well spoken by good actors..."(Barrault).[1] "Mouvement avant la parole", said Decroux. Speech comes out of movement. It demands more of the actor than simply to think colorfully in literary terms. Creativity is not the priority of the writer or director.

The actor's training, must provide him with an understanding of the actor's physical process and the ability to weave his way through the labyrinth of creative development, taking on and solving questions as they arise. There are ways of arriving at this knowledge that seem to me to be meaningful, generous, sensible and exciting. Others strike me as wasteful, indulgent, and self-centered. The process must be one of embracing and rejecting. In working through the process there will be moments when everyone, the actors, teachers, and directors will sit up and ask, "Why?" Why did that moment make sense? And when answers are found, they must be kept close and not forgotten.

"All these tasks are for the senses and his (the actor's) training is of a physical kind" (Brecht).[2]

Notes

INTRODUCTION

1. This thought reflects the fundamental principle on which Decroux based his ideas on theatre and the subsequent training of the actor. It is, therefore, found, reoccurring and developing, in various discussions of his work. With this in mind, I would like to refer readers to the interviews with Decroux contained in *Mime Journal, Numbers Seven and Eight*, Thomas Leabhart,(ed.) Allendale, Michigan, 1978.

Unless otherwise stated, all quotes from Etienne Decroux, in this book, are taken from my notebooks. They are based on classes and discussions I had with Decroux over a period from 1959–1978, as well as discussions and notebook exchanges with other Decroux students in these years. Decroux constantly developed and reworked ideas, which accounts for similar thoughts used in different contexts or with slightly changed wordings found in other sources.

2. Throughout the book I have used the word "physicality" to refer to the complete physical being of a person or character. I am inferring to the essential characteristics that make up the physical image or physical presence of someone: the sense of "presènce physique" in French or "die körperlichkeit" (corporeality) in German.

I am aware that, in English, "physicality" often carries with it certain negative connotations—a sense of "baseness", for example . It has become an antonym for "spirituality". I assume that this reflects a certain Protestant morality. One's physical being, one's "physicality", is an important concept for the actor. It is in this context that the use of "physicality" must be understood.

CHAPTER ONE

1. Barrault, J.L., *Reflections on the Theatre* (London: Rockliff, 1951), p.102.

CHAPTER TWO

1. Pisk, L., *The Actor and His Body* (London: Harrap, 1975), p.9.

2. Brook, P., *The Shifting Point* (London: Methuen, 1988), p.43.

3. Barrault, J.L., op.cit., p.20.

4. I'd like to refer readers to two sources that develop these thoughts in more detail: Willett, J., *The Theatre of Bertolt Brecht* (London: Methuen, 1977), esp. pp.143–186, and Braun,E., *The Director and the Stage*, (London: Methuen, 1987), pp.163–179.

5. Popov, O., "Russian Clown" in Rolfe, B.(ed.) *Mimes on Miming* (London: Millington, 1981), p.164.

6. Decroux, E., quoted in Lecoq, J. et al.(eds.) *Le téâtre du geste:mimes et acteurs* (Paris: Bordas, 1987), p.66.

7. Davis, R.G., "Method in Mime" in Rolfe,B., (ed.) op.cit., p.207.

8. Barrault, J.L., op.cit., p.31.

9. Ibid, p.23.

CHAPTER THREE

1. In order to delve further into the ideas of Etienne Decroux, please refer to *Mime Journal, Number One* (Fayetteville, Arkansas,1974), and *Mime Journal, Numbers Seven and Eight* (Allendale,Michigan,1978), both edited by Thomas Leabhart.

2. Brook, P., op.cit., p.107.

CHAPTER FOUR

1. Barrault, J.L., op.cit. p.114.

2. Ibid, p.168.

3. Brecht, B., "A Short Organum for the Theatre" in John Willett (ed.) *Brecht on Theatre*, (New York: Hill and Wang, 1964), p.204.

4. Berger, J. *Art and Revolution*,(London: Writers and Readers, 1969) p.50.

5. For more information please refer to: Brecht, B., "Short Description of a New Technique of Acting Which Produces an Alienation Effect" in John Willett (ed), *Brecht on Theatre*, op.cit. pp.136–147.

6. Losey, J., quoted in Milne, T., *Losey on Losey*, (Garden City, New York: Doubleday, 1968), p.104.

7. Willett, J., *The Theatre of Bertolt Brecht*, op.cit. p.97.

CHAPTER FIVE

1. Decroux, E., quoted in Leabhart, T., "The Origin of Corporeal Mime", *Mime Journal*, Numbers Seven and Eight, op.cit. p.15

2. Decroux, E., "Each Art Has Its Own Territory" in Rolfe, B.(ed.), *Mimes on Miming* op.cit. p.106.

3. Lebreton, Y., quoted in Bourquin, D., "To Talk of Mime..." in Rolfe, B.(ed.) *Mimes on Miming* op.cit. p.4.

EPILOGUE

1. Barrault, J.L., op.cit. p.84.

2. Brecht, B., in John Willett (ed.), *Brecht on Theatre*, op.cit. p.243.

Appendix One

Exercises for the Preparation and Development of the Actor's Body

WHEN TEACHING PHYSICAL EXERCISE to the actor, the tutor must incessantly relate the work at hand to the demands of the theatre space. The connection must be clear in order for the student actor to understand how and why these exercises serve his craft. It is essential that all body work and movement exercises be seen as a means towards solving physical problems specific to the actor's needs, whether in the creating of theatre or in performance.

Great care must be taken to assure that body work never becomes isolated from the rest of an actor's work. Links continually must be made to other parts of an actor's training: to the voice work (e.g., posture, breath); to the music work (e.g., interactions, "conversations" through music and rhythms); to acting (e.g., offering-accepting, listening, following clear objectives, clarity of image, economy). It is exactly these links that most excite theatre students.

For this reason, I am opposed to body work and an actor's movement work being separated. A class that begins with body work should be allowed to continue into improv work, which addresses questions of space awareness, interactions, sustaining physicality, and physical imagination. At other times, problems relating to the rehearsal situation directly at hand should be addressed in class (e.g., when working on character development, or when an actor is faced with specific technical problems such as running down stairs, or falling on one's face).

Often, there is an initial excitement with body work, as the students find that they can do remarkable things with their bodies, and that their feet and legs really will hold them up. However, after a while, the hard, continuous, slow, somewhat tedious, work may get them down. They aren't flying after six weeks. Their bodies are reacting more slowly than their brains. Constant reminding of process and goals must take place. Progress and development must be illustrated. At this stage there may be a certain amount of carrying the students along. Slowly, bodies do change and the impossible appears obtainable.

The concept of "good and bad pain" must be understood. Pain is there to let us know all is not right. Gradually, how far to go—a "helpful pain"—becomes recognizable. Pain must always be used as a guide. I would rather not talk about "passing the pain barrier," as one "new circus" director put it to me, but rather about making use of pain: learning to "listen" to it, and responding properly. The student must learn about his own body—its weaknesses and strengths. In conjunction with the tutor, he must find the best means of working on "problems." I find this a very subjective process.

Alignment, awareness, control, coordination, relaxation, strength, and flexibility are all necessary to the actor's work. There are many movement techniques that address these needs. Some are more useful to the actor than others. I would hope that this book will encourage most readers to rethink, take on, discard, and add to their previous techniques and experiences. All the while, they must concern themselves with the actor's needs, as opposed to those of the dancer, the acrobat, the office worker, the athlete, or others.

My work is based on mime techniques and dance techniques, but is influenced, as well, by physical therapy exercises, specific gymnastics, and yoga work, and, to some extent, the very personal working methods developed by certain physical theatre directors. Through the years I have tried, adopted, discarded, and developed work, often in order to answer needs as they arose. Sometimes I have put a specific type of work away for a later moment. I would urge readers to do the same.

The following exercises are meant to serve as a sample, a point of departure, and not a regime—please! The order in which things are done is of utmost importance. Great attention must also be given to the care and thoughtfulness with which the exercises are executed, be they elements from a mime warm-up, a ballet barre, on Chinese opera training techniques.

The "motor of a movement" (Decroux) must always be present. Every exercise must begin by identifying with clarity, its inner rhythm —a rhythm that begins deep inside the body, emerges through it, and ultimately causes the body to move. Rhythms must not be externally imposed. The actor must follow the dictates of his breath. It is his movement that must sing!

Part One: Warm-Up Exercises— Preparing the Body for Work

The warm-up, whether commencing a movement class or immediately preceding a rehearsal or performance must be done with great precision and attention to detail. The objective of the work is to get the body sensitive and alive—prepared for the demands that follow. In order to have a responsive instrument, and be able to avoid injury when working, a proper warm-up is essential. The order in which exercises are done must be understood and adhered to. Alignment, breath, relaxation,—the elements that make up *"the zero"*—are the basis from which the work must start and can develop. Often I will ask the actors to sing or speak during the more strenuous exercises. This insures that breathing will take place and enforces the concept of using the minimum energy necessary to execute a movement.

Though the body warm-up is primarily concerned with preparing individual bodies for work, the warm-up should be done with the entire company or class and not individually with the actors going off into their own corners. The reason for this is to nurture the need for a constant awareness of space and all that is happening within that space. In this way, the actor will learn consciously to avoid bumping and kicking his colleague, as well as becoming aware of the rhythms and breathing of the others. He will be reminded of his role as part of the whole.

In place, standing:

1. *Zero: Establishing the neutral.*

2. *Gentle stretches and relaxation for the entire body:* Pay special attention to warming-up the spine thoroughly. Remember to emphasize the need to identify and use the minimum energy required for the execution of each movement.

3. *Gentle joint warm-ups:* Warm-ups for the hips, knees, ankles, feet, back, shoulders, wrists. Each exercise should contain both a stretching and contraction of the muscles. Special awareness should be placed on the turnout.

4. *Large stretches of the entire body in all directions:* Forward, side, back. At first, work with isolated movements, building curves, etc., and then progress to gentle bounces or gentle swings and drops, etc.

5. *Slow, precise deep knee-bends in second and first position* (in that order!): Work on deep knee-bends, using explosive or soft impulses in combination with balance work and leg stretches.

6. *Large exercises for total coordination, balance, back and leg strength:* Lifting legs, developés, etc.

7. *Large, standing stretches for legs and pelvis:* Try bounces in second; falls which change a movement's direction and/or transfer the weight; lunges; barre stretches, etc.

8. *Exercises for energetic coordination, controlled speed and balance:* Involve movement of the whole body. Make use of the space, using exercises that involve a change of direction, change of rhythm, etc.

Note: A good deal of time and care must be given to exercises numbers 2–5.

Sitting or lying on the floor:

9. *Hand stretches, hand positions, arm work:* Experiment with rhythms and impulses. Insist on the difference between architectonic movement and movement that begins from an impulse.

10. *Back stretching and strengthening:* Pay special attention to alignment when the torso is in unusual positions, e.g., on the oblique. Always be aware of working the vertebrae, one by one, when reestablishing verticle lines, when doing undulations, etc.

Bounces, in curves or with a straight back, should always be done gently. Never pull the body over with the hands on the back of neck or by having another person pushing. One must work with one's own back strength!

11. *Lower back and inner thigh strengthening and stretching*: When addressing these problems, I've found various physiotherapy exercises most helpful.

a. Lying on one's side, the head propped up in the hand, it's weight resting on the elbow, lift the legs together and hold them there for eight breaths. Slowly lower them. Repeat. (Special attention must be paid to keeping the body in a very straight line.)

b. When lying in the same position, as above, bend the top leg and bring it in as close to the chest as possible. Keep the body straight and the bottom leg extended on the floor. Holding the body and upper leg in place, kick the straight leg backwards. The accent is always out. Repeat.

12. *Leg and torso stretching*

13. *Leg strengthening*: Work on the turnout, on leg and feet awareness, on positioning.

14. *Stomach, lower back exercises*: Avoid, at all costs, sit-ups while lying on the floor. All movement involving the lifting of legs should be done from a position where the body is propped up on the elbows.

15. *Relaxation exercises*: Some relaxation exercises combine muscle awareness with relaxation, while others are totally or almost totally passive. Clear decisions must always be made concerning the purpose of the relaxation exercise and when and how it should be introduced into the process.

a. Try melting: Using the lowest level of energy needed, raise and lower the body from standing to lying positions. Study closely the use of weight.

b. Lying on the back, try isolating parts of the body in both contraction and relaxation: the lower back, the right or left shoulder blade, the upper arm, the hands. Try pushing these parts of the body into the ground and then releasing.

16. *Relaxation and stretch (yoga based)*:

a. *Salute to the Sun*- my version of an often used, yoga-based exercise, adapted here for the actor warming-up for rehearsal, performance or movement class. I find it an excellent way to finish a warm-up, as it leaves the body relaxed, but centered, prepared for the work to follow.

Find a neutral, relaxed zero, in a parallel second position. Pay attention to correct, relaxed breathing.

Inhale and lift arms high, above the head. Keeping the feet well grounded, stretch the entire body upwards, so that the back is lifted in a high arch. Be sure that the shoulders remain relaxed and down. Most important, take care to always breathe properly from the diaphram.

Exhale and let the body hang over the feet, bending from the pelvis, hands on or near to the floor.

Inhale and simultaneously bend the left leg while placing the right leg back in a lunge position, arching the head, chest and waist backwards. The right leg must be as long and straight as possible. The left heel remains on the floor. The hands are either firmly pushing into the floor, or lifted above the head, (forming part of the arch, the body lifted, from the waist, up and back).

Exhale and bring the left leg back to join the right leg. At this point the body is in a press-up position, (that is to say, in a long, straight line from the heels to the back of the head).

Inhale and in a swooping movement, the knees, then chest and then chin touch the ground as the body is pushed forward, up and back. The final position reached is one of the hands pressing firmly into the ground, the head, chest and waist forming an arch backwards, with the pelvis and legs resting on the floor.

Exhale and bring the right leg forward, to a position where the forehead is touching the bent knee. The left leg remains behind, as always, long and straight.

Inhale and, remaining in the same position, lift the body up and back, so that there is a long arch backwards of the head, chest and waist. The left leg remains long and straight, and the hands, either firmly, on the ground or lifted above the head.

Exhale and bring the left leg forward, keeping it straight, while the right leg is also straightend, bringing the body into a position where the feet are now together in a parallel second position, and the body is bent over from the pelvis, the head touching the straight knees.

Inhale and roll up the body, continuing until the arms are lifted high over the head in a long stretch, the entire body arched up and backwards.

Exhale and return to the original zero position.

Repeat the entire series of movements, substituting the left leg wherever the right leg moved first.

b. *The Cat-* a comprehensive exercise designed by British actor and movement director James Hennessy. This exercise, when executed in it's entirety, taking both the time and care it requires, simultaneously centers, relaxes, warms-up and prepares the actor for workshop, rehearsal or performance situation.

Shake out and organize the body.

Find the zero position, relaxed and neutral, the body straight and organized, the weight centered, and evenly distributed on both feet.

From the "zero", shift the weight forward onto the toes.

Keeping the body straight, shift the weight backwards onto the heels.

Gently sway the body back and forth, between these two positions.

Return to the centre, and the zero position, weight evenly settled over feet.

Feel the free, relaxed muscles. Breathe easily.

Continue with a breathing and stretching cycle.

Standing in the zero, breathe out.

Breathe in, and letting the breath lead, rise on tip-toe, arms stretched, above the head.

Breathe out, and bending from the pelvis, flop over, (heels firmly on the ground and   the head near the knees).

Repeat the sequence two or three times.

Begin to work on the spine.

Slowly, roll down the back, beginning from the head, vertabra by vertabra, until the head is near the knees.

Hanging from the pelvis, breathe into the stretch.

Placing hands on the floor, walk away from the feet.

Arrive at a standard push-up position, back flat.

Keeping the back flat, lower the body to the floor, (chin on floor, arms by side, shoulders on floor).

Cobra position: lift the head and chest off the ground. Turn the head to the right, centre, left. Repeat.

Sphinx position: raise body higher from Cobra position, until weight is resting on the elbows. Turn the head right, centre, left. Repeat.

Cobra position with arm support: raise body from Sphinx position, until arms are straight. Turn the head right, centre, left. Repeat.

Gently lower the body to the floor.

Raise the body to the push-up position.

Hand walk back to the feet, keeping heels firmly on the ground.

In this rounded position, ease nose gently towards knees a few times.

Hand walk back again to push-up position (back straight).

Work on flexibility in the lower back and pelvis

From the push-up position, swing the hips, in a circle, clock-wise, four times

and then anti-clock-wise, four times.

From the push-up position, lift the legs up in back several times, first the right leg and then the left leg.

As above, only this time kick (gently) the right leg out to the side several times, followed by the same movement with the left leg.

Keeping the hands firmly on the ground, pounce through several times, bringing the forehead to the knees, and then returning to the push-up position.

From the push-up position, scoop through,(nose, chest, waist, pelvis), until the body arrives in the Cobra position with arm support.

Relax

Pull the bottom back to a position where one is sitting on the heels, head over the knees, arms out in front. In this position, rest.

Sit up, on heels. Bend each wrist, forward and back. Bend each foot, forward and back. Flex the face.

Work on the hands, first clenching and then spreading the fingers. Work slowly, and gradually getting faster, feeling as if the fingers are being thrown outwards, into space.

Work on leg and back strength.

Focussing on a fixed point at a 45 degree angle, push the pelvis through until the body is raised to a kneeling position, the back arched, the hands on heels.

Return to a resting position, sitting on the heels.

Roll forward into a head stand.

Push, again, through the pelvis, arriving, for a second time, into a high arch stretching from the knees to the tip of the head, (this time, without support from the hands placed on the heels!)

Rock forward and backwards seven times, going further back each time.

On the eighth time, arch back so far that the head reaches the floor.

Breath into the position.

Roll over onto stomach, lying flat on the floor.

Lift both the arms and the legs off the floor. Hold the position and then gently lower.

Repeat three or four times.

Roll onto back, hugging the knees tightly to the chest. Gently rock, forwards and backwards.

Hugging knees to chest, pull the lower spine (coccyx) off the floor and then lower it, eight times.

Stretch out legs.

Bend the right leg, bringing the right foot up, next to the left knee, while keeping the foot flat on the floor.

Arc the knee over the left thigh, bringing the right pelvis off the floor; arc the back. Bring the foot back to the floor. Repeat eight times.

Repeat, as above, with left side.

Lying on the back, bring both knees up, keeping the feet flat on the floor.

With the knees and feet together, arc into a "bridge" of the lower spine. Return.

With knees and feet apart, arc into a "bridge" of the lower spine.

Then, in the same position, lift body up into a high arch, touching the nose to the ground, and then lower the back, vertabra by vertabra.

Rest, hugging the knees to the chest.

Continue to work on the back, arriving in the Candle position.

Lie flat on the ground.

Swing the legs over the head and relax. Place hands behind lower back for support.

Lift the legs parallel to the floor. Open and close them eight times.

Repeat with legs raised to 45 degree angle.

Repeat with legs at 90 degree angle. (Always support lower back with hands.)

Lift the body onto the shoulders. Rest in this position, always paying great attention to the breathing.

Stretch, letting straight legs hang over the head.

Rest, hugging knees to chest.

From this position, turn the head to the right and twist the knees to left shoulder. Bring the head and knees back to the center, and repeat the movement, this time turning the head to the left and twisting the knees to the right shoulder.

Move on to more strenuous leg and body stretches.

Straighten both legs. Role over backwards, keeping the right leg straight. Settle the body into a long lunge, the right leg back, and the body sitting on a bent left leg.

Twist the upper body and sit on the floor, the right leg remaining extended, but now out to the side. The left leg is still bent, in front of the body, pulled in close. The arms are in a "T" position, out to the sides.

Stretch the arms up and over the straight leg. Return to center. Repeat.

Twist the body to face the straight leg, the knee pointing upward and the foot flexed, also pointing upward. With arms up above head, lift the body up, out of the pelvis, and over the leg. Return the body to an upright position and repeat several times.

Bend the straight leg across the bent leg, bending it so that the right foot is flat on the ground, next to the outside of the left thigh. Hug the knee to the chest. Twist the body to the right, so that the left nipple touches the right knee. Twist the body in the other direction. Place left hand on floor. Push up, as the body twists, lifting it up onto the feet, while completing a 180 degrees turn. Finish standing, weight on both feet, facing the opposite direction.

Walk six paces forward. Come to standstill, feeling the muscles free, breathing easily.

Keeping knees straight, go into a head stand and then a forward role. Rest with the knees hugged to the chest.

Rolling over into backward roll, end with the left leg out backwards, the body resting on the bent right leg, in a "lunge"
position.

From this position, repeat the last series of exercises, this time stretching over the left leg.

Relax and breathe.

Stand with the legs spread wide apart. Keeping the legs straight, bend over and move into a forward roll. Finish lying on the back. Relax.

Stretch through body, arms above head. Roll over onto stomach.

Move into push-up position. Back Flat!

Hand walk gently towards feet.

Hang from pelvis, without hand support. Freedom check.

Roll up through spine, vertabra by vertabra.

Gently lift shoulders up and place on rib-cage.

Check that the weight is evenly placed on feet. Sway gently forwards and backwards.

Check that the muscles are free and that the breathing is easy.

Part Two: Developing the Instrument— Body Techniques for the Actor

The following order need not be followed:

1. *Isolation exercises*: These exercises involve either moving parts of the body independently from the rest or moving all parts of the body together, as one unit (the total body). Work in all directions and on different angles, using a variety of inner rhythms, e.g., explosive, sustained hums, "breathy", vibrating, etc. Remember that a caress starts before the touch: it begins with the inner impulse, that comes out through the vibration of the arm, etc.

   a. Try moving independently the head, neck, chest, waist, pelvis, as well as the total body, in inclinations, translations and rotations. Work in all directions. Try combining inclinations, rotations, and translations to create a variety of designs in space. For example: rotate the head to the right, incline it to the right, incline it forward, and then translate it forward. Return to the zero through the same path, simply reversing the order.

   b. Try moving the extremities independently, e.g., the fingers, hands, arms, feet, legs. Move them one at a time in a variety of combinations.

   c. Try isolating individual muscles in different positions, e.g., while standing, sitting, lying etc. Isolate muscles at the back the neck, in the upper arm, etc.. Work on contracting and releasing as well as vibrating isolated muscles.

   d. Study exercises based on the rules of diction, i.e., one part of the body moves at a time, much as we speak one word at a time: The eyes pull the head, neck, chest, waist, pelvis, total body, etc. Move in combinations of rotations, inclinations, and translations. Work carefully in all directions. Always use the inner monologue: "I see" causes a rotation,"I look" causes a translation, and "I react" the breath dictates the direction of the movement. Perhaps the dramatic situation will cause the actor to move towards what he sees, or perhaps, to the contrary, he will lose interest and return to his neutral.

2. Inclinations, Translations and Rotations: Moving isolated parts of the body and/or the total body.

   a. Try the following inclinations:

- forward, back, side, in all positions.
- "eiffel towers": with a variety of rhythms and designs; with descents and rising to and from the "demi-tour eiffle", etc..

"eiffle towers": imperceptibly moving from second position to the oblique (the audience never sees the moment of departure or the moment of arrival onto the oblique—at one moment they simply realize that the actor is inclining).

- curves: forming the curves (forward, side, back); descending with them, etc.

b. Try the following translations:

- forward, back, side.
- pushing, pulling; being pushed and pulled.
- tug of war (a study of pulling and being pulled).
- seeing, hearing, smelling; the eye, the ear, or the nose will always lead the action, pulling the rest of the body along, and by doing so create a direct line in space to the object of its attention-that which it has seen, heard or smelled. This will happen whether the person is approaching or backing off from the object, whether the person is losing interest in the object, or the object is loosing it's intensity, etc.

Try *seeing* an object, and being pulled to it by the eyes.

Try *hearing* a sound that gets closer and further away; gets louder and softer; disappears and returns.

Try *smelling*—the nose leading in a direct line to or away from the smell.

When working on the senses, use a variety of directions, levels and lines, i.e., forward, side, back, up and down, in direct lines and on obliques.

c. Try a variety of rotations:

- descents.
- pivots.
- others.

3. *Three-dimensional exercises*: These exercises consist of combinations of inclinations, translations, and rotations, using both isolated movement as well as movement of the total body. When the basic movement has been created, add further elements, such as the shifting of weight, or pivots, or changes in the lev-

els, i.e., descents and rising, etc. Three dimensional movements are large movements, requiring a sense of the body in its surrounding space.

4. *Falls*: Try falling forward, sideways, and backward, as well as in spirals, to the knees, or to a position flat on the floor. Working on falls serves several pedagogical purposes at once: a) learning about safety and the avoiding of injury; b) as a way to concretely illustrate the use of isolated movements in the theatre space, e.g., inclinations to create curves; c) as an exercise that makes use of newly identified coordination within a dramatic context. The process must be taught with emphasis on precision —one movement at a time, safely, and in detail. Actors must understand how and when to trick the audience. The audience, for example, must never see the "soft-landing" (landing one knee at a time), but it must be there. Falls must be faked if they are to be accomplished, night after night, without injury. At the same time, they must always be believable and look natural. They must be practiced and mastered, until the moment when it becomes habit to avoid one's knees, one's hands, one's elbows, and instead to fall on one's shoulders, or pelvis, shifting the weight at the right moment. In the first instances, mats and "spotters" should be used in the teaching of falls. The process must be clear: the student is learning to fall believably, without taking risks.

5. *Undulations.*

6. *Counterweights*: Push/pull.

    a. Try walking the dog.

7. *Exercises for the transferring or shifting of weight.*

8. *Exercises involving the changing of intensity*: These exercises are concerned with the use of intensity in movement to create the feeling of presence and the illusion of weight.

    a. Create resistance in space. Notice that some things create more resistance than others. Look at walks, defining the differences between light and heavy walks.

    b. Create resistance in space with the hands. For example, keep the fingers very straight and try squeezing the fingers, one at a time, together with the thumb, as if there is a tremendous force between them which will not let the finger and thumb come together. Each time the finger and the thumb do manage to meet, relax the hand, return it to a neutral, and begin again with the next finger.

c. Push out to create a large circle through space with the hands and arms. The circle can be in any direction: in front, above the head, to the right or left side, or over the shoulder. With maximum intensity, push the space away. After the initial explosion, continue pushing until the circle is completed and the intensity has withered away. The movement ends at the point where it began, and, at the same moment the neutral is reached. With a new impulse, begin pushing in another direction.

d. As above, push through space, only this time add the hand exercise as well. Now the fingers and the arms begin and end their movement at the same moment. They both begin with a maximum of intensity and return to a relaxed zero. This is an exercise in the study of two lengths: of space and of time. Movements of the same time and intensity, but with very different lengths, begin and are completed at the same moment.

e. Move or push through space as if moving through salt water or oil or against the wind.

f. Move illusionary objects of different weight and sizes, e.g., pouring water, or lifting a rock, etc. The illusion of weight is caused by creating resistance in space.

g. Push against space, as if trying to move it! Push up and down, high and low, forward or behind, under legs, and over right or left shoulder.

All work on intensity should include discussion of personal tensions, such as grimace, raised shoulders, claw-like hands, etc.

9. *Exercises in immobility*:

a. Individually or in a group, gradually bring a walk to a complete stop. The actor must identify within himself:

• *the weight*: the feeling of pushing into the ground, the weight slightly forward, ready to act; a secret relaxation always present.

• *the regard*: where one is looking; the focus.

• *respiration*: the breath.

• *tension*

• *living immobility*: action in stillness.

b. Arrive imperceptibly to the state of immobility. The audience never sees the moment when the actor comes to a rest.

10. *Inner rhythm exercises:*

a. Study explosive and lyrical movements (smooth and synco-pated). Move from a standing position to the floor and back again, repeatedly rising and lowering the body. Change from explosive, angular movements to round, lyrical movements at the signal from an outside person (tutor/director).

b. Study inner rhythm as the cause of a movement. Move-ment responds to the impulse from the breath. A sharp impulse, running through the body like a shock (a gasp, for example) will cause the arms to respond in a larger or smaller movement, in one direction or another, depending on the intensity of the shock, and the direction it provoked. Try, for example, standing in a mime's fourth position, facing right. Following the impulse caused by an inner monologue, turn 180 degrees (moving through a second position) and arrive to a fourth position facing left. Return, with the same impulse. Create a series of differing dramatic situations. Though the movement created will be the same design in space, it is the cause of the action that will give it its dramatic value. Try different inner monologues, e.g., "I feel so peaceful. It's nice to be alone. What's that noise in the other room? It's getting closer! Help!"; or "I'm so tired of waiting. I wish he'd come soon. Oh! You were behind me all the time!"; or "I'm so, so exhausted. The kids are being just too quiet. I must go see what they're doing...if they're alright. Oh, kids! Come on kids! No!," Find others. The movement in itself (the turn) is simple. It is the reason for turning that will dictate how it is done, and therefore, determine the dramatic statement. The actor must learn not to block the impulse, but let the breath, caused by the inner monologue, manifest itself. Making the invisible visible!

c. Study animals in great detail. Find and then define the rhythm of an animal and how this rhythm manifests itself in the animal's movement. Find words that seem to describe an animal's characteristics, e.g., a small animal and "hesitancy"; a dog and "bouncy"; a bull and "powerful"; a cat and "unpredictable" or "supple","graceful","egoist"; the horse and "steady"; the monkey and "agility". Other animals to think about might include the swan, shark, cock, octopus, and eagle.

d. Look closely at the idea of the "escargot". Here we are considering the element of hesitation or surprise, which then causes the recoil or retreat. These exercises are a study in touch—of the head, the hand, etc. Perhaps the ultimate of

Decroux's wonderful animal descriptions was of the snail: "The poet who comes out of his shell and then returns after having seen the world!"

e. Understand the neutral. What rhythms does "neutral" imply? Why does "small and direct" make the audience listen?

f. Work on exercises involving a change of direction; the explosive moment of change, in walks or other movements, that serve to catch the audience unawares.

11. *Exercises on being grounded*: Feel and identify weight. For the actor this means taking the space and creating one's presence in that space. Identify the feeling of pushing down into the ground and simultaneously sending the body's energy up and out.

a. Vary the levels of heaviness, while repeating specific movements or exercises. Always sustain, to a degree, both weight and the energy going up and out. Think perhaps of Matisse's "Icarus"—large, heavy, solid legs and arms reaching upwards...respectful of the ground upon which we walk, while reaching for the heavens.

12. *Lecoq's seven levels of tension*: When crossing the length of the space, the actor identifies the physical feelings caused by a steadily increasing level of tension. Perhaps more than anything else, this is an exercise in breath awareness. This or similar exercises can be found time and again in differing circumstances. I find that there is no absolute concerning how or when they should be done. What is helpful is to make sure that the problem the exercise is addressing is clear before it is begun.

a. The seven points are:

(1) almost an absence of tension—as found in a baby, or drunk

(2) very relaxed—a laid back quality

(3) a neutral

(4) lightness—like the sigh: airy, floating, a feeling of up

(5) explosive—a quality of fire

(6) high tension—the quality of melodrama

(7) complete tension—which results in immobility

Go the length of the space, and then return, reversing the process; i.e., the actor is going from points 1 to 7, and then 7 to 1.

b. As above, only this time speed up the process.

c. Create a narrative with two people; e.g., two people explore a deserted house, or (more complicated) a relationship.

13. *Walks*: Walking through space, allow various outside elements to affect the body, e.g., heat, cold, exhaustion, sickness, and age. What happens to tension levels?

Part Three: Space Awareness Exercises—Group Work in the Theatre Space

1. *Follow the leader*: As the group walks in a circle, one person is designated "leader". He finds a particular movement (walk, jump, run, series of falls) that continues to propel him forward. Everyone in the group must copy his movement, paying special attention to the rhythm of the movement, to its use and placement of weight, and to its every detail. What exactly are the neck, the fingers, the palm of the hand, etc. doing? They continue to walk in the circular pattern. After a time, the leader calls out someone else's name, who then becomes the leader and finds another movement for the group to imitate and study. The exercise continues until everyone in the group has had a chance to be leader.

2. *Figure Eight*: Using the entire space, the group walks in the form of a very large figure eight. At the point of crossing, one person passes through the space at a time. In order to be able to do this, everyone in the group must be moving in the same rhythm—a rhythm that can never be broken. The actors must maintain an acute awareness of the space. After a while, speed up the movement to a trot, a run, etc.

3. *Walking the lines of space*: An exercise for awareness of oneself and others in the space. The actors, one by one, enter the space, walking to a rhythm set by the tutor/director/outsider. The actors must walk only on horizontal or vertical imaginary lines, "squaring their corners", etc. There are no curves no diagonals and there must be no overtaking one another. Never changing the rhythm, the actors must avoid one another. This implies that they must be aware of where everyone is in the space and always ready to change direction. After a while, the rhythm may be changed (perhaps sped up to a slow run). Again, the rhythm is always set by the outsider (the tutor/director, etc.). The actors

will find that they must look straight ahead, using peripheral vision, and must never look down at the imaginary lines, if they are to avoid collisions with their colleagues, and if they are eventually to develop relationships with other people in the space.

a. The actors block one another by creating obstacles, i.e., they lie down whenever and wherever and the others must never step over (or on) them, but by changing direction avoid them.

b. The actors walk quickly along the "lines of the space." At a signal from an outsider (tutor/director,etc.) all stop in place—"on a dime"—and immediately close their eyes. The outsider goes to each actor and quietly asks him, to point to and, in a whisper, identify the person nearest to him. After this is done the actors open their eyes to see if they were right, or not.

c. Following on from the previous exercise, the actors continue, at a quick pace, to walk the lines of the space. They must now take special care to keep track of the person whom they have just pointed out as being closest to them. At the clap of the outsider's hands, all stop, shut their eyes again, and indicate the whereabouts of the person of whom they have been especially aware during the exercise.

d. An imaginary magnetic field is created, situated in the centre of the space. The actors are pulled, very gently, by this field and are no longer able to use the whole space. Rather, as the force seems to get increasingly stronger, they are pulled towards the center and into a smaller and smaller area. They must continue to walk at the same rhythm and follow the same rules, until they find themselves in a very tight knot, still walking the lines of the space. There will be a tendency for the actors to want to repeat their movement patterns. They must be encouraged, however, to keep the same rules going as when they were working in larger areas and their patterns must still be dictated by other people's movement and use of the space. They will eventually find that they must use smaller steps!

e. Still walking the lines of the space, create a pattern using ten steps forward in any combination, and then repeat it walking backwards. As always, use the entire space and continue to follow the rules of only walking on horizontal and vertical lines. Each person in the group must be very aware of the space and be able to begin and end his pattern in the exact same place. The actors will notice the tendency to take smaller steps when walking backwards.

f. Try the same exercise as above, only this time with the eyes closed!

g. Later on, when studying physical interactions, the actors working in pairs may try to develop relationships with one another while walking the lines of the space. The relationship and interaction should be allowed to develop, until the moment when the action causes both of the actors to exit, together or separately, from the space. It is necessary to follow the rules of the exercise at all times, i.e., never breaking the rhythm, nor stopping, nor speaking, nor moving off the horizontal and vertical lines. When finished, discuss what each actor understood to be his partner's objective, i.e., what he understood his partner wanted from him. Then discuss, with those watching, what they have understood to be the actors' objectives. Only then, ask the actors themselves to define what they had wanted from one another. It is often interesting to repeat the exercise with the clearly defined objectives and see what occurs.

4. *Walking the Quadrate*: ("walking the lines of the Union Jack", as I have heard this exercise described). Imaginary lines are created in the space, forming a cross, an "X", and the frame along the sides, back and front of the space (the lines of the "Union Jack"). Five to nine actors are placed at intersections, where the lines meet. There are nine possibilities in all. From these points, the actors enter into the space (much as in the former exercise), in the rhythm dictated by the outsider. However, no more than one actor must ever enter onto or be on one line (between two of these points) at a given time. The actors may change directions only at the points of conjunction. They may never stop and must never lose or change the rhythm. They must not pass one another, nor go backwards. This exercise develops awareness of the space and others in that space.

Later on, this is an excellent exercise for learning to create the sense of crowds in the space, using the elements of distance, of the lines of the space (obliques, direct lines, etc.), and of groupings. In a television play, Beckett used this design in space to create a complete, albeit short, play.

When working on the exercises numbers 2,3 and 4, which are concerned with lines in the stage space, keep in mind that *oblique* lines create distance and vagueness; that a horizon is created by looking up and over and never directly forward; that *direct* lines create closeness and collusion with the audience; that *proximity* and the feeling of closeness can be created with a direct look (at great distance) as well as by physical closeness; and that, when wishing to create *focus*, there are specific places and lines in the space that create more powerful focus than others—the "warm spots" of the space, as they are called.

5. *Tangle*: The actors, in groups of seven to ten, hold hands (firmly) and make a circle. The hands must remain, from the beginning to end of the exercise, in the same position. The group proceeds to get themselves thoroughly entangled, going over and under each other's arms and legs until the group is a tight knot. When the knot is formed, the group is asked to make eye contact with everyone in the group.

a. Now make the group as small as possible, huddling into a tight, low bunch, and then, again, make eye contact.

b. Now make the group as wide and spread out as possible and then make eye contact.

Try other possibilities of using the space, and then:

c. Very slowly, return to the original circle by repeating, in reverse, the journey that the group took to tangle themselves up in the first place. All should end up exactly as they started.

It is very important, while working on tangles, for everyone to move slowly, aware of their own whereabouts and movements, as well as those of the others. Great care must be taken to be conscious of others' bodies and how much they are being pulled, so that arms are not pulled out of sockets.

6. *Mirrors*: The actors work in pairs, mirroring one another's movement. The actor who begins will determine (lead) the movement until there is a signal from the outsider (tutor/director, etc.) to switch, at which point the other person becomes leader. Later, the pair should change leadership by one player simply taking over—interrupting, so to speak—the movement of the current leader. Movement should include use of the whole body, moving through space in all directions and at all levels.

The actors will find it necessary to maintain eye contact in order to maintain the high level of concentration required in the exercise. They will notice that the movement becomes lost if they look around or if they attempt to anticipate. They will also notice how important it is for the leader to be very clear and precise.

a. Change the rhythms, moving from slow to fast; lyrical to explosive; etc.

b. The leader adds to the above exercise an accompanying sound, which his partner must also mirror.

7. *Machine (with sound)*: In this exercise, the actors enter the space, one by one creating together, through sound and movement, the atmosphere of a working machine. As each actor goes up, he creates a repetitive movement or gesture and complementary sound, which he must then sustain throughout the exercise. One by one, the actors add to the "machine", finding movements that are a logical development of the movements already in the space. For example, if one actor's repetitive movement consists of lunging forward and returning, a complementary movement might be jumping into the space each time the first actor has emptied it. Each actor must sustain his own inner rhythm and sound throughout the exercise.

When the "machine" has been built, it suddenly begins to go wrong, speeding up frantically, until the moment when it simply breaks apart and collapses.

8. *Throwing and receiving gesture (silent and with sound)*: Two lines are formed facing each other, with seven to ten people per line. The first actor at the head of the line begins by throwing a gesture to the actor across from him, causing a response from that actor. The feelings coming out of that response will be the cause of another gesture that the second actor directs towards the actor across from him on the diagonal. This actor now responds to that gesture, which in turn causes another gesture, which he will then throw to the actor across on the diagonal from him. And so the gestures continue, and the action zigzags down the line. When the end of the line is reached, the action simply continues to zigzag back up again and goes up and down the line for quite a long time.

The actors must be allowed the time to relax into the play, in order to be able to respond and physically react to the offers, without planning and constructing gestures. Action must cause action. Each gesture must be a credible response to the previous gesture (no matter how absurd or silly the movement may feel). Actors should be discouraged from using illusionary objects (such as balls) and encouraged to let their physical imagination soar. It is easy to fall into aggressive gesture. Encourage, therefore, the exploration of subtle feelings. This may result in very minimal gesture, and the actors will notice the importance of clear movement if a response is to be expected. It often takes a group quite a while to get into the exercise, but once they do, it can be kept going for half an hour or so. Add sound. The sound is simply a further physicalization of the impulse, an extension of the "gesture".

9. *Shock-resonance*: Working in partners, one actor throws a well-directed gesture (from the fist, the hand, the head, the back, the elbow, the shoulder, the foot, the knee, the hip, the bottom, etc.) to a specific point on his partners body. Throughout the exercise the actors will never touch. In fact, as the exercise develops, the blows may be sent from a greater and greater distance, until, finally, they are directed from across the room. The throwing of the blow causes, in turn, the receiver to recoil with a shock, leading from the point at which the blow was aimed (much as would actually happen at the moment of being knocked or hit). A head is aimed at the stomach, or a palm of the hand to a cheek, or an elbow to a back, etc. Both actors continue the movement caused by the explosion, taking it to it's conclusion. The movement will wither away until it comes to a stop. The first gesture is a shock, an explosion, much like a gasp in the breath, and is therefore small and powerful. The receiver of the blow reacts more or less simultaneously, also with an explosive movement a gasp, and a quick retreat. That movement, too, is carried out to its conclusion. When both movements have come to an end and both actors are in a moment of neutrality, the person who has been hit (from whatever position he now finds himself) throws a well-directed blow back towards his partner. The first actor then responds, and so the series of movements continues. There is always a shock, which in turn causes a shock and a retreat. All movement must be taken through to its conclusion, before the other lashes out. The exercise is looking at where an impulse begins and the differences between an internal and external motor of a movement; e.g., striking out or being struck; looking at or being looked at. Actions must never be allowed to stop midway. It is like the gong, that, after the initial strike and sound, simply dies out. As the actors at no time actually touch, their intentions must always be exceedingly clear.

When doing this exercise, the actors must always keep in mind that it is the shock that causes the resonance. At first, it is perhaps best to work with gestures based on direct blows, as this makes the cause and effect easier to define. Later, the exercise can be done with two actors sitting on a bench, the explosive movements originating through furtive glances.

This exercise takes a great deal of concentration and intent listening to one another: As there is never physical contact, the distances can be very great, and the rhythms are much slower than in a real fight. The actor must learn to suspend the realities of the real event. When the rules of the game can be finally applied to stealthy glances, the work comes into its own.

10. *Puppets on elastic*: One actor pulls or manipulates another actor's movements by pulling him by an invisible string. At first, imagine the string tied about the waist (later attached to various other points of the body, such as the chest, a leg, an arm). Then try to imagine more than one string attached to several points of the actor's body at once. Try having both actors, simultaneously attached, e.g., a hand attached to the other actor's foot, etc. The actor controlling the strings dictates not only the movements, but the rhythm of the movements as well. The two actors must breathe together as one. It is the breath that will allow them to feel one another's presence in the space.

Try attaching the imaginary strings to the four hands. The actors will pull and be pulled, changing from manipulated to manipulator as they will. When one takes over in the position of leader, his intentions must be extremely clear.

11. *Darkness, a study in hesitation*: The actor or actors explore the space as if they were in complete darkness. Explore the difference between being sighted and not seeing anything because of total darkness and being blind in the same darkness. Define the difference. Look at the energy levels involved, at the focus; at the physicalization of the movement.

12. *The essence of a dream*: Ask the actor to take a personal dream and to find one gesture or movement and one sound that will represent the essence of that dream.

13. *Balance and support*: These are exercises that demand the physical give and take of actors working in close contact with one another. *The actors must be very warmed-up before attempting any of this work.*

a. Working in partners, one actor manipulates the leg movement of his partner. While one person stands in a first position zero, the other very gently begins to lift his right leg. It must be kept absolutely straight and correctly turned-out at the hip. The rest of the body must remain in its aligned, neutral position. The leg is lifted as high as it will go. The point of this exercise is not so much for stretching, as for teaching awareness of other people's bodies—their physical possibilities and limitations. The actors must be working with extreme sensitivity, in order to feel the moment when the muscles begin to resist. Because the leg is being supported, it will be completely relaxed, and this is yet another thing of which the supporter must be conscious. When the leg is as high as it will go, the supporter moves backwards, carrying the leg forward, resulting in both legs being stretched at the same time. If the leg is able to go high enough, it can be rested on the supporter's shoulder as he moves back, and he can then help balance his partner by holding his hands. The torso of the actor who is being supported must remain straight and aligned, as his supporting leg also moves forward onto an oblique. The leg is then brought back to the upright position and then carried to the side (always maintaining the correct hip position), and again all the weight is resting on the supporter. Special care must be taken here to keep the body aligned. As the supporter moves out and away from his partner, the legs of the person being stretched will be increasingly on the oblique. When the maximum stretch for that particular person is achieved, the leg is brought back, so that the body is returned to its upright position and is then carried back to the front, where it is gently placed in the original first position zero. Repeat with the left leg.

b. Working in partners, the actors try as they continuously move to never stop touching. They begin by standing side by side with their fingertips touching, and then let it flow. As they mirror each other, one or another part of their bodies must always be touching; e.g., their heads, their pelvises, their knees, their hips, their elbows.

c. The same exercise as above, only this time the partners remain holding on to one another throughout the exercise. Moving continuously, they give each other their weight, pulling away or leaning onto one another, using one another to find their balance. Finally, they find their toes touching. They bring the soles of their feet together and lift the knees high until they reach a point where they can straighten their legs in front of themselves, forming a "V". They will need to lean backwards in order to have space. When they have found their balance, they will let go of one pair of hands and turn to face the audience balancing, with their legs in an upside down "V", their feet pressing together and their hands holding on tightly.

In the last two exercises, the tutor/director/outsider may, in the beginning, call out which parts of the body are to touch. After a while the actors should work in absolute silence on their own, one movement simply emerging out of the previous movement, enjoying a new level of physical communication and understanding.

14. Minimum points of balance: The actors, spread out in the space (always beginning from a "zero"), begin to move, trying to use the minimum points of balance necessary to execute their movement. This means, for example, that if they can let themselves down to the floor with one leg, on tiptoe, they should not be using two feet and one hand. Their movement develops continuously, slowly, gently, never stopping. All movement comes out of the preceding movement, simply emerging and is in no way preplanned (i.e.,"now I will stand on my head", etc.). The actors' objective, all the while, is to constantly search for the minimum points of balance needed to keep the movement going. Allow the exercise to continue for ten to fifteen minutes. It is exhausting, but with time the actors begin to stop repeating the same, familiar movements and to realize their bodies' possibilities. However, the exercise must stop when they begin to lose, from tiredness, their concentration and control. If someone does lose concentration, he must pull himself out of the exercise until he is again centered. Discuss what happened, what didn't, etc.

a. Following from the above exercise, allow the individual actor, as he moves through space, to make use of another's body, in order to gain the balance necessary to complete the impulse of a movement. For example, it might be possible to raise the body while balancing on one hand, if the back and the weight is resting on another person's back. A sense of offering and receiving will develop as the actors become aware of each other in the space and learn to trust one another, both in the receiving and giving of weight. All rules of support and balance must be adhered to, i.e., weight must only be given when one is sure the supporter can carry the weight (it is, in fact, the supporter who offers). At the same time, it is important that the actor doesn't go about looking for someone to support. Rather the movement continues to flow, developing out of what has gone before. At first actors must only work in pairs, which will change as the impetus of the movement moves the actors along to someone else.

b. The same exercise as above, only now the actors are working in groups of four to six people. At times, the actors will find themselves working closely with the whole group (four people being the support for one person, etc.). At other times they may be working in pairs, or alone. Again the movement, and therefore the groupings, must be allowed to evolve. The movement never stops, nor is it planned or anticipated. All the while, the actors are using the minimum points of balance necessary to execute their movements.

This is wonderful exercise, creating in the actor a sense of physical confidence and the ability to develop his physical imagination.

15. *Dictated number of points of balance*: In this exercise the actors are working in groups of three to five people. It is better, at first, to work with three people and only later, enlarge the groupings. The outsider (tutor, director, or other) will call out a number from one to ten. The actors will then build a human structure, with as many points of contact to the floor as the number that has been called out. For example, "three" might result in two legs and one head touching the floor and the rest of the bodies being balanced or suspended, and a "one" might result in a structure built on the back of one person, etc. "Points" may include, feet, hands, heads, shoulders, bottoms, backs, knees, etc. Obviously, the lower the number, the harder it is to balance. There should be no talking, just experimenting until a structure is found that the actors can hold and balance. Have the groups watch each other and notice how rich and varied the possibilities can be.

16. *Trust exercises*: These exercises are less about how to trust someone else physically in the space, than about how to be trustworthy when working with others. They are based on the assumption that though one person may be working in the unknown, the others around him are in control of the space and the movement in the space.

a. In this exercise three actors work together. One person stands in the middle, and is pushed and caught by the other two, who stand on the outside facing the person in the centre. The middle person, keeping himself very straight and never letting himself relax or break, falls forward (like a board) towards his partner, who catches him with both hands at the front of his shoulders. The middle person, remaining passive, is pushed again very gently back towards the other colleague, who will catch him with both hands on the shoulder blades. He is thus gently pushed back and forth several times. Important rules must be observed. Firstly, the catchers must test the weight that they are about to catch by being quite close to the person falling, so that the fall is very small. The catchers must stand with one leg behind the other, so that they are free to move with the weight, letting it take them back. The centre person must always remain absolutely rigid, while the catchers must always be in a position that permits them to move with the weight they are catching. If the person in the centre is frightened of falling (especially backwards) all three people should be positioned close together. Only allow the distance to widen when everyone is confident of the weight each is catching and the person falling has identified the physical feeling of remaining rigid.

b. This exercise is similar to the one above, but taking it one step further. Here we use five catchers standing in a circle and one person in the centre of the circle. The centre person is gently pushed from one person to another, never knowing to which person he will be directed. All the catchers must be ready to catch (take the weight) at any moment. Before a catcher pushes, he must make eye contact with the receiver. This exercise can be done very quickly, but the eye contact of the catchers and the rigidity of the centre person can never be relaxed for a second. The center person can try eventually to keep his eyes closed during the exercise.

Groups should observe other groups work. They will note the dramatic possibilities of these last two exercises—both comic and frightening. For example, a tipsy character falls about, landing into everyone's arms, or, in another example, the character is menacingly pushed about and manipulated in a fight scene.

c. An actor runs and leaps into the arms of ten others. The ten actors form two lines of five each, and facing their partner (the person across from them), they cross and link arms by grabbing each other's wrists. The actor will then take a running leap into this nest. He must take care not to overshoot the nest and must land in the middle. Those catching must be prepared for the weight, by standing in a position with a good base, one leg somewhat behind the other, so that they are able to move with the weight.

This exercise should only be done after a great deal of support and balance work.

d. The same as above, only this time the actor is leaping from the height of a table into the nest made by the ten actors below him. The actor falls face forward. When first doing this exercise it is always good to have a crash mat under the arms of the catchers.

The work on the actor's instrument (Chapter Three) and the work on an actor's corporeal expression (Chapter Two) must be presented and taught in a simultaneous and interdependent manner. it is this way that the task before the young actor gains in clarity.

Appendix Two
Becoming the Physically Articulate Actor: Exercises for Using the Instrument

THE FOLLOWING EXERCISES are grouped according to the role they play in an actor's training. There is, of course, a great deal of overlap and often an exercise will address more than one pedagogical problem at a time. The purpose of the exercises is to clarify the role of the body in acting and to provide the actor with the means to use his instrument theatrically. Some exercises will seem more relevant to a specific moment in an actor's training than others. An exercise will often serve different needs at different times in the developmental process. At first, for example, an exercise may be used to enable the actor to understand the possibilities of space, and, later on, as a means to find how best to communicate in that space. As control in support and balance work develop, exercises originally used in offer and response work may be expanded and applied to work on physical interactions.

There is a definite pattern in understanding and assimilating the work. At times, the exercises will seem unfathomable to the actor; but if relentlessly continued they will begin to make sense, and the struggle becomes clearer. The moment of discovery, the moment when one truly understands the purpose behind an exercise, is always very exciting. It is important to have other actors watching, and to follow the work with discussion. When an actor or group of actors finishes an exercise, I always ask those working and those not working to talk about what they saw. What happened or didn't happen for the actors? What did we, the audience, understand? Why? This work is as important for those watching as for those doing. It is important that students learn to watch each other and analyze what they see.

Mask work early on (as an aid to the actor's training, and not as a theatre skill or form) is an excellent way of making it possible for the students to see vividly what the body can do, or often is not doing. It tends to illustrate clearly what one is looking for and where one is heading. I find it better than video for making this sort of analysis.

A mask is very revealing and is a wonderful method to clarify what we mean by "economy of movement." It is very useful in illustrating how each movement serves a purpose and has a dramatic value. The power of stillness, the potentiality of the physical attitude and image, the use of focus and rhythm, etc.— all become self-evident. The actor's need to concentrate and to refrain from all excess becomes unavoidable. "Pretending" (to see, hear, and feel, etc.) is more blatant than ever, and increasingly unacceptable—in fact, almost impossible for the audience to tolerate. Real use of, and contact in, the space is demanded. A mask forces an actor, in early character work, to find a body. He can no longer hide behind words and charisma. Every movement counts and is part of a dramatic moment. Often it is in mask work that students first discover the poetry of "the minimum," and of "the essence." They find there is simply no need for words. It seems impossible to cheat. In a way, this gives one an added freedom.

I have separated the work into types of exercises and then listed them in order of difficulty, marking work suitable at the beginning level with a "B". Again, these exercises are to serve as a point of departure, and are designed to give an idea of how one should be working. They address problems of concentration, of awareness, of risk, and can be very exposing. The working atmosphere must be one of calm support, but never support for the easy way out, such as laughing at every gag or irrelevant bit of business.

Part One: The Actor's Body as Explicit Communicator—Increased Awareness of an Actor's Physical Possibilities

1. *Walking exercises* (B):

a. The actors, working in groups of five to six, walk diagonally across the space, one after another (when one has crossed, the next begins). The first time across, they walk "naturally", which is to say, they try to walk as they normally do. They are asked to cross the space many more times, finding as many characters and their walks as possible. The actor is not looking for physical types, such as fat, or tall. Rather, he is discovering the physicality of people representing a variety of experiences and backgrounds, all with their own self-image. The actor must, as always, have made clear decisions, i.e.,"Who am I"?" Where am I going?" and "Why"? After having tried several walks, the actors are asked to find a character and his walk that is as different as possible from his own self-image. When the group has completed the exercise, those watching are asked to analyze what they have seen. What are the characteristics found in each of the actor's own walks? How and where do they carry their weight? What image is conveyed? What are the predominant rhythms and mannerisms? What interactions are there between one part of the body and another? Which part of the body leads? Which of the actor's characteristics remain with him throughout all of his walks?

b. The actor walks across the space, allowing specific parts of the body to lead. What images does he create? (Decroux and Lecoq inspired). For example:

the head = intellect

the chest = heart, dignity

the stomach – greed, sloth

the pelvis = sexuality

the feet = ego, comedy

c. Walking across the space, the actors try to be colors. This exercise is riddled with problems. Colors can mean different things to different people. It is a very subjective exercise. It is similar, however, to much of the work on elements, when an actor is asked to identify within himself, earth, fire, air, and water. The actor is required to define concretely, through physical feelings, impressions that have, until then, always remained abstract, or, at best, have been based in emotional responses.

d. Walking through space, the actor allows the senses to motivate an action. One sees, one looks, one touches, one tastes, one hears. The external influences that we experience, cause within us an internal reaction. A wall is warm. A taste is bitter. The path along the edge of a cliff is dangerous.

The actors, working individually, must identify, (using sense memory as a basis) the physical feeling which the action has caused. They then must take the time to allow that feeling to manifest itself physically. They must be careful not to hurry and not allow themselves to block or cut short a moment. Rather they must enjoy the moment and let it develop. Try repeating these moments, rediscovering the physical feeling that has been previously identified.

e. Walking in a circle, the actors pass through a series of varying experiences. The outsider calls out a gamut of emotional and physical feelings, e.g., joy, fury, terror, courage, indifference, disappointment, jealousy, love, expectation, hot, cold, burning, foul taste, etc. The actor, while continuing to walk in a circle, must find, identify, and sustain these feelings by creating a situation within himself that creates an emotional reaction corresponding to the word. The key to this work is the inner monologue. The actor's whole body must be responsive to all that he is feeling inside so that, without words, these feelings can be communicated to his audience.

This is a excellent exercise for understanding the possibilities of inner monologue. It can be done with large groups walking in a circle.

f. In this exercise, the actor is finding and exploring levels of tension. Moving across the space, the actor explores the rise in the level of tension that occurs as one moves from slight fear to the fear of death. When he comes to the end of the space, he turns around and reverses the process, until he arrives to the same point in the space and the same emotional level where he began.Repeat the same exercise, expanding it to other emotional responses in specific circumstances, e.g., high energy to exhaustion; low status to high status, etc.

2. *A study in open and closed movement*(B):

    a. The actor begins by finding a specific physical attitude or image, such as sitting on the floor, or standing with arms reaching out in front of him, or kneeling with his head resting in the hands. The outsider gives a series of contrasting commands that evoke contrasting sentiments: "Come here!" "Go away!" "I want this!" "I hate this!" "Stay here!" "Remain there!" The actor sustains his attitude, and through the breath and inner monologue, develops the situation. How does the body change? How does the body respond to feelings of greed, of altruism, of egoism, etc.? Notice how the same gesture can convey opposite meanings. What is the key to the exercise? *The chest, as conveyer of emotions, is the key.* Openness begins with the chest, as does closedness. When clear, the subtlest of movement becomes enormously expressive.

    In the mid-1980s, at the Barbican Theatre, London, J.L.Barrault used a similar exercise to explain what he meant by "expression corporelle." At the time, he was shouted off the stage by the English audience, because he was speaking in French, and because they wanted him to replay his famous film character, Baptiste. It was a great sadness that so few people actually listened to what he had to say. I, myself, have never heard or seen the actor's physicality demonstrated with such clarity, and such passionate love for the actor's work.

3. *Familiar action* (B):

Find an action.

Find and add a sound that goes with the action.

Find the source of emotion that is caused by the action, always sustaining the previous steps of the exercise.

Find an accompanying inner monologue that reflects the previous steps. At first, say it out loud.

Bring the action back to silence, retaining the clarity of the action, the emotion, and the thought.

4. *Creating familiar and unfamiliar actions in the performance space* (B):

    a. Pick up a book. It may be interesting, boring, exciting, erotic, etc. Eventually the reader falls asleep. As always, the action, the feelings, and the thoughts must be explicit to those watching.

b. Walk away from the enemy. There is a level on which one continues to fight the enemy, physically, emotionally, etc., even after he and the danger are gone.

c. Enter the space and begin a simple and clearly motivated action. The actor must choose a space with which he is very familiar, e.g., one's bedroom, one's living room, one's church, the underground, etc. The action must be familiar to the actor as well, e.g., going to bed, brushing teeth, lighting a candle, taking out a book to read, etc.

d. Repeat the exercise of establishing a familiar action, but this time in a space that is unfamiliar to the actor, e.g., a religious ceremony, a prison, a disco, etc.

These exercises in establishing space and action are excellent exercises, later on, when working with masks.

5. *Enter—Statement—Exit* (B):

a. In this exercise, the actor must create a space and establish, with clarity, a presence and action in that space, i.e., who he is in the space, and what he wants from the space. From the moment he enters until the moment he exits, his motivations must be clear to the audience. They must know the reason for his entrance into the space and why, eventually, he leaves.An excellent exercise for beginning character work, and with masks.This exercise is also an excellent rehearsal vehicle, for helping to define a character in a specific space.

Exercises becoming more complex!

6. *Animals: finding essential qualities of animals and transferring them into people* (Decroux inspired):

a. The actors must define in great detail the physical characteristics that make an animal what it is. What makes a cat different from a dog? What makes a lion different from a domestic cat? What are the physical feelings specific to their physicality? The actors should begin by studying the inner rhythms of the animals, and looking closely at how they use their weight, etc.What are the animal's essential qualities?

b. Apply these qualities to human characteristics. Find words that help develop this process, e.g., cat—the unexpected and slinky; the bulldog—strength; the terrier—determined; the rodent—hesitant, etc.(Refer to Appendix One, Part Two, Exercise 10.) After one has worked on the individual animals, put the animals into situations that will cause interactions, e.g., one cat meets one dog; or one cat meets a pack of dogs;

a turtle meets an ant-eater; or a giraffe meets a bird, etc.

c. Keep the word that has been found, and now, having defined it in relationship to an animal, transfer it to a character. As above, put characters with specific animal characteristics together in situations and allow interactions and relationships to develop. An excellent exercise for early rehearsal.

7. *Finding essential qualities of plants and transferring them to human qualities*:

a.Take a plant and observe it through all the senses. How does it feel, smell, taste? What does it looks like? What does it sounds like when you bite into it, etc.? Find words for these qualities, e.g., light, spongy, pure, cool, prickly, fuzzy, slimy; or "pretty on the outside, watery on the inside", etc. Think of plants used to describe people, e.g., "cool as a cucumber", "hot as a pepper", "a peachy personality", "fresh as a daisy", etc. Using these qualities, apply them to characters.

8. *Passage to opposites*:

a. Walking, in a straight line, the length of the space, the actor goes from a feeling of kindliness to extreme anger, reaching the epitome of the anger at the same moment he reaches the end of the space. Sustaining this feeling, the actor turns around and goes back across the space, this time moving from the point of extreme anger that he has achieved, to the original feeling of benevolence.

The actor must take great care never to jump from one feeling or degree of a feeling to another. Rather, he must let the feelings emerge, one developing into the other. The key here is inner monologue.

b. The same exercise as above, but this time go from rich to poor. Explore the struggle to keep dignity. Always return to the original point in space and situation.

c. Using familiar characters (specifically one the actor is working on at the moment), take him on the same or similar passage. This will provide a great many clues about the character's behaviour, etc. Refer to Brecht's *Herr Puntila*.

9. *Establish a being, a mood, an atmosphere, a place, and then explore*:

a. Explore and discover an object, such as a box, an animal, a warm blanket, a piece of clothing, etc. Establish it and then share it with the public. Leave it perhaps with reluctance, etc.

10. *Inner Monologue exercises* (The following three exercises are

excellent with mask):

a. Enter. See something. Want it. Examine it. It's funny. No, it's horrible. It disappears. Search for it and find instead, two of the same object. Confusion! Which one is wanted? Develop the inner conflict.

b. See an object. Take it. It reminds the character of something else. Look at the object and have an idea.

c. Take something the others aren't to see.

11. *Compression of Time*:

a. Twenty-four hours into three minutes: identify the essential movements of the action(s). Time is created with rhythm and space. One must be careful not to simply jump from one action to another, nor to lose the essential. "Intensity replaces time"(Decroux).

b. Sleep to sleep: notice essential differences in types of sleepiness and tiredness, etc. Despite the repetitiveness of certain movements, the essential of the action can be very different. Identify it.

c. Count one's enormous piles of money or one's few pennies. Establish the action and then speed it up. Herein lies the key. notice that this is possible only when the very essential of a movement remains.

d. In a theatrical context, cross kilometers in thirty seconds and then cross a short distance in the same time.

e. Birth, maturity, old age and death—in place. Marceau inspired!

12. *The senses*:

a. Touching: Caress with the cheek. Let the moment develop. Find reactions such as surprise, hesitation ("escargot"), etc. Afterwards, touch and explore with the hand or foot or back, etc.

b. Touching: Walk into a wall. Find the element of surprise (relaxation to explosion). Explore the wall. Is it smooth or rough? Is it hot or cool? Does it have holes on it? Is it transparent? Find and define what the wall means to the character. The wall does not have to be an illusionary wall. A nondescript real wall can be used. The actor then endows it with its characteristics.

c. Seeing: Explore the difference between seeing and looking. The actor sees something. He looks and then reacts. Notice the use of oblique and direct lines, i.e., the difference in seeing something concrete and "seeing" an idea, etc.

Part Two: Improvisations for Clarity of Interactions

1. *Actor and the bishop* (Viola Spolin exercise): A group of ten to twenty actors stand in a circle. Two actors standing next to each other begin, one in the role of a "bishop" and the other in the role of an "actor". Simultaneously, they turn their backs to one another and address the person standing to the other side of them, "I am a bishop." (or "I am an actor",etc.). "A what?" comes the reply. " A bishop." "Oh, a bishop." That is the whole dialogue and must be learned (well!) by everyone. The person having just been addressed, now turns to the person on the other side of him and begins, "I am a bishop". This is followed by the next person down the circle saying, "A what?" "A bishop." "Oh, a bishop." etc. Counterclockwise the same process is going on with "I am an actor." Eventually the actors will come to the situation where a "bishop" is talking with an "actor" and the following dialogue will evolve: "I am a bishop". "I am an actor". "A what?" "A what?" "A bishop." "An actor." "Oh! a Bishop." "Oh! an actor." They then turn, with their new personas, to their neighbors on the other side and begin again. It is also possible in the meetings for one person to be carrying on two conversations at the same time, i.e., they are presenting their one persona to one of their neighbors, while receiving the other neighbor's persona. It can become very complicated, which is why the dialogue must be very clear in everyone's mind!

Why this exercise? I like it because it allows the actors to use their imagination when physicalizing their character. This, in turn, determines the interaction and relationship that they develop together through their "conversation". The exercise works only if the actors are willing to take risks in exploring the many facets of actors and bishops and their possible interactions. I have seen the same "game" played with an orange and an apple as a concentration exercise. I believe, however, that the point of the exercise is to discover the vast range of possible physicalities attached to one character. This, in turn, helps define for the actor what we mean by an "actor's imagination".

If there are a lot of people doing the exercise, it is possible and fun to add more characters, so that you have several pairs going around the circle at one time.

2. *Family portraits*: Six to eight actors line up, their backs to the audience. They have previously decided among themselves,

what their relationships to one another are, i.e., mother, father, daughter, son, grandmother, grandfather, son-in-law, aunt, uncle, family dog or cat, etc. At a signal (hand clap) from the outsider, they all simultaneously pivot with one movement and freeze, facing the audience—posing like a family portrait. Each character has followed the impulse coming from his objective, e.g.,"I want Grandma to rest", etc. From this picture, the audience must be able to see and understand certain family interactions. Perhaps the wife has turned her back firmly on her husband, and all of her attention is focussed on her smallest child. Perhaps the lovers have eyes only for each other, allowing two of the younger children to fight. Perhaps the son is teasing the cat, etc. With another clap of the hands, the actors pivot back to a "zero," their backs again to the audience. They may remain positioned where they landed after the first clap. Perhaps they are on their knees or sitting. They may be, for example, standing in front of or behind another character, etc. But they must return to a neutral state. With the next clap, they again turn to the public, developing further the relationships that were begun in the last freeze. In the series of claps and freezes that follow, the characters and the interactions should broaden. It is even possible that a bit of narrative may appear. The primary purpose of the exercise, however, is for the actors to work for an increased awareness of one another's motivations, which in turn frees them to act and interact.

3. *Conversations in movement*: A group of approximately five actors scatter themselves about in the space and finding their "zero" position are ready to begin. The primary rule of the exercise is that one person moves at a time, much as one person speaks at a time in a conversation. The only exception will be if two or more actors are moving together, as a "unit". In this case their movement is much like the sigh or murmur or laughter of a crowd. To begin with, the outsider will give each actor a number, and he will call the numbers out (most likely not in consecutive order, but rather in the order in which the action is unfurling). When a number is called, the corresponding actor must take an action—carefully finding a dramatic reason behind every movement. The first few "goes" will require the actor(s) to set up the dramatic situation, but once this has been done, the previous actions will determine how the actors move. All movement is in response to what has or has not happened before. An actor may find, for example, that he has very little to "say", and his movement will be minimal or even almost imper-

ceptible. On the contrary, he may put forth a whole diatribe involving a long series of movements. After a time, the outsider will indicate to the actors that they are on their own and will cease to call out numbers. They must continue as they have begun, making statements and respond to statements as they would in a verbal conversation. For example, actor "A" might be relating to actor "B" and the interaction might be something like this: "A" to "B", back to "A", back to "B"; "C" interrupts, which causes a response from "A"; this causes "D" to turn his back on the whole thing, and seeing their chance to get out of the situation "E" and "B", together as a unit, join "D", etc. Because the actors are moving, one person at a time, everyone is forced to move with absolute perspicuity. Every statement must be ended with the clarity of punctuation, i.e., a full stop, exclamation point, etc. Even when the statement ends in a questioning, or withering away of movement, there must be no question in the minds of the other actors as to whether or not the actor is finished. The actors who are not moving must remain immobile, but with an inner breath, a "living immobility." Here again, one can think in terms of a conversation. It is similar to the moment when one person is speaking, and the others are silent, but still very much a part of the action or conversation. Quiet and still, they are simply listening. Remember "action-packed stillness"!

Until the actors have become used to this exercise, they often find it quite difficult. It poses many problems for the actor to solve. They must, for example, be very careful not to allow themselves to use pantomime (gestures which replace words, e.g., pointing for "there" or shaking the head for "no", etc.). They must avoid using illusionary objects. They must be aware of the "stage picture" and not block or cover their colleagues. Their awareness of the stage space must be very acute. If they find that their back is turned to the action, they must have trust in their colleagues to bring them back into the conversation. Every actor must be very clear in his motivation, in order, to be clear to the other actors. Everyone must know what everyone else wants from him! Being still, and listening is one of the hardest things for the actor to do. He must listen to the others' thoughts and emotions—to their breath! The primary objective must be clearly defined and the entire ensemble must go for it, and yet avoid all superfluity.

This exercise requires from the actors their utmost generosity—and when it works, it is a great joy! After the rules of the exercise have been mastered, the exercise can be expanded.

For example:

a. Define specific characters and/or relationships and place them in specific situations.

b. Use specific props or bits of set, e.g., a chair or a table.

c. Set the primary objective (the same objective for all the actors): "I want that chair more than anything in the world, but, equally important, no one must know how much I want that chair!" This is one of my favorite exercises, because it poses the problem of two, seemingly contradictory, objectives.

d. See a thing that causes an idea to follow—a Conversation in Movement on seeing and looking. Try the reverse as well, i.e., looking at an idea that affects how one sees a thing. Three or four characters watch the same image, but their thoughts and point of view may be very different. Try three dissimilar characters, all initially sitting at a table, e.g., a philosopher, a cleaner, a youth, etc. Try as well three seemingly similar people, e.g., the philosopher, the dreamer, the writer, and perhaps the waiter who dreams.

Remember the rules concerning differing lines in the space and how they effect the images created. Looking down, on an oblique for example, gives the illusion of studying detail, while looking up on the oblique gives the impression of seeing an idea. Remember that things are looked at with direct lines, and ideas are seen on the oblique, etc. Experiment. This is a Decroux exercise from which I have seen more than one piece evolve.

e. Try a Conversations in Movement with two people sitting on a bench, etc.

Conversations in Movement are, in my opinion, probably one of the most important exercises I have included in the book. They are exercises that I would include in almost every prerehearsal warm-up.

4. *Creating interactions:*

a. An actor enters the space with a clear and simple action. He freezes his action. One by one other actors join him, each with a well-defined motivation. As the actors develop the situation they must follow all the rules of a Conversation in Movement, i.e., always one person moves at a time unless a unit, etc.

b. All the actors sit in a large circle. One actor will enter the circle from outside of it. As he enters, he is in the midst of a very clearly motivated action, i.e., where he has come from, where he is going, why, what he wants, etc. In mid-action the actor freezes. At this point, another actor, who has been sitting in the circle, gets up and enters the space and the action. His objective will be in response to the first actor's action. He freezes in mid-action, thereby creating a clear tableau of an interaction between the two. Gradually the two actors bring their tableau back to life, developing the interaction until it reaches a point that causes the actors to leave the space. For example, an actor runs into the space and trips. He is clearly being chased and is frightened. In the midst of his fall he freezes. The second actor has a lot of choices—perhaps he is a killer, or a policeman, or someone wanting to help the tripped man get up, etc. His acting decisions will determine how the situation progresses. This, in turn, will determine how it will end. Perhaps it ends with the policeman making an arrest and taking him off. Perhaps the first man must continue to try to escape from the killer, etc.

When the actors are finished, the action is analyzed, first by the actors participating, i.e., what did they understand to be the other's objective, etc., and then those watching discuss what they saw and understood. The two actors should repeat the exercise—with the same characters and the same motivations, trying to make the situation physically explicit. Their inner monologue must be very precise. Here, again, we have an excellent exercise, for illustrating what we mean by physically articulate acting.

c. This exercise creates interactions that involve a fall. Two actors set up a situation where one actor causes the other to fall. For example, one stabs or shoots the other in the back. Or one grabs the other to embrace him and, in the process, causes him to trip. Or, perhaps, one bumps into the other and they both fall over, etc.

The actors must have defined who they are, and where they are in the space, as well as where they have come from and where they are going at the moment of entering. This must be equally clear to the audience.

The techniques used in creating the falls must not be perceptible. The actor dictates to the audience what is to be seen. The exercise is one that demands exact timing from the actors if the action is to be credible.

Again, they must breathe together. Often the actors are surprised at what they are capable of doing. As legs go flying over heads, they realize that it is the awareness of one another and the space, along with physical control, (rather than physical strength) that allows the dramatic moment to be successful.

5. *Meetings:*

a. Two people enter simultaneously from opposite sides of the space and meet in the space. How their meeting evolves will be in response to their intentions, i.e., what they want from each other will depend on who they are and what they want for themselves. For example, one's intention might be the need to force the other to leave the space, etc. Use colorful language such as "cunning" to help find the rhythm. Try using animals with the same or opposite rhythms, e.g., a turtle and a giraffe.

b. Two people enter into the space, from the opposite sides and move diagonally forward. At the point of meeting, one of the actors will take the lead and circle the other. With his actor's decision to take the lead, he has created status, and, in doing so, a dramatic moment. With this relationship established, the actors must find a motivation that will cause them to exit in opposite directions. How and why they leave the space will depend on the interaction they have created.

c. Two actors see one another. They react. They study each other. They are looking at and being looked at. At one moment their eyes meet. There are purposely no "givens" at the beginning of the exercise, i.e., whether they know each other or not is up to the actors to decide at the moment of seeing one another, etc. What then happens will be an illustration of what Lecoq describes as push/pull dynamics.

d. The same exercise as above, but add a third person, who enters at the moment when the first two people's eyes meet.

e. These are meetings in which a reversal of dynamics/roles, take place. Opposites such as leader/follower, officer/soldier, weakest/strongest, etc. meet. In the process of meeting, their roles reverse. The exercise can be done so that the characters actually change roles, i.e., the soldier becomes an officer. Or they can remain the same character, but one must gain status over the other, i.e., the soldier becomes the more powerful, etc. This process should be continued so that there is another reversal, and both characters end up back in the positions in which they started. When they have reestablished their original person, they find an action that will take them both out of the space together or separately.

As the change takes place, the entire process must be visible to the audience. The actors must take their time to identify physically, the feelings taking place as their status changes. They must go through the entire gamut of the rise, or the diminishing of status, etc. and then change back again. *It is through clarity of physical feelings that one is enabled to find clarity in physicality.*

f. The same exercise as above, but using first animals and then characters with animal qualities. In the first step, a dog meets a cat, or a cat meets a bird, etc. Then, either one or both of the animals take/s on the characteristics of the other animal. For example, a bulldog becomes cat-like in a bulldog's body, etc. In the third step, a character with defined animal characteristics takes on the characteristics of another animal, i.e., a bouncy, gruff dog-like character becomes hesitant, like a small rodent.

g. Again, extending exercise "d," concentrate this time on achieving clarity of attitudes (essences), which must be based on an actor's clarity of who the character is and what he wants. Working in pairs, essential opposites meet and respond. Gradually their states of being are switched. Try for example: proud/humble, angry/happy, afraid/secure, serious/jocose.

Situations for meetings are endless and provide an excellent milieu for applying rules that will help in defining the situation. There must always be clear motivation for the character's exit as well as entrance into the space.

6. *Trying to hide, to be invisible* (a group exercise, following the rules of "Conversations in Movement"):

a. "I want to be invisible," but no one will allow it. As a group, or individually, the others resist the attempts of the one actor to be by himself, apart from everyone else. At times they resist on purpose, at other times it is by accident.

b. As above, but this time the motivation is subtly changed, "All I want is to be left alone."

7. *Tableaux*: A group of five to eight actors begin by creating a still frame of an action or situation. Each actor is very clear about who he is and what his role is in the situation. A typical situation might be, for example, a bank scene: with tellers, people depositing money, children waiting for their parents, the bank manager, bank robbers, etc. With a signal from the outsider, the ensemble brings the scene to life and the action devel-

ops, until there is another signal from the outsider, this time to freeze. The narrative progresses through a series of freezes, actions, freezes, etc.

At each freeze, those watching should be able to identify the interactions of all the people involved in the scene. Don't forget that a lack of interaction is an interaction of sorts and certainly can be a strong dramatic statement. If, at the moment of a freeze, the actors realize that they should or could be somewhere else, in order to take the clarity of the image further, they should move. Likewise, an actor might ask his colleague to change his position, in order to make their interaction clearer, etc.

This exercise is an excellent one for an actor's awareness of others in the space and for developing a sense of all the possibilities offered by a specific dramatic moment. In some ways, the actors are working as directors, solving problems of form and content. At the same time they are defining their relationships and physical actions. For this reason, it is a very good exercise for early on in the rehearsal process. The exercise can be done in silence, with abstract sounds, or with improvised speech. I would suggest that the first few times it be done in silence.

8. *The Outsider*: Following the rules of a Conversation in Movement, the group of actors, establishes interactions, making use of a curtain or screens. In this way, they can make themselves visible and invisible to the audience. This can be an important element in the actor's relationship to the audience. One character establishes himself as the outsider—he is always outside the action, looking in. Yet his presence is always felt. Explore the possibilities.

Part Three: Exercises for Imagination and Creativity

1. *Creating atmospheres*: Following the rules for Conversations in Movement, define a space, e.g., a waiting room, a train platform, a laundromat, or a museum. The actors must make something happen, by making actor's decisions. What do they want from other people in the space, etc.? It can be helpful, when doing these exercises, to use aids such as colorful words, or animal encounters.

2. *Situation exercises*: These exercises are designed to serve as a point of departure for the actor, and provide a stimulating basis from which the actor's imagination can take off. The actors must have clearly defined for themselves who they are, what they want—individually, and as a whole. Only then can the catalyst of the situation function.

a. Inner monologue, i.e.,"I see. I'm interested. No, I'm afraid. But, it's funny. No, no, it's horrible. It's gone. I want it. No I don't! What's that? It's coming. It's going over me! Wasn't really anything anyway."

b. "All mad, except me."

c. A letter is lost.

d. Something of value is broken.

e. Through work one becomes exhausted, e.g., a mannequin, a doctor, a mother, etc.

This can be an immensely complex exercise. It is a study in getting down to the essential of an activity, as well as a study in compressing time. It requires the actors to use inner monologue and physical feelings in order not to jump from one two-dimensional attitude to another.

f. A phone call is received.

g. The long-awaited letter arrives.

h. The actor takes an object that reminds him of something else.

i. Slow recognition of someone or something, which touches upon a feeling. This exercise points out, among other things, that one does not have to be big to be clear.

These last two exercises are from Decroux and are wonderful, because an actor simply cannot cheat in them and be successful.

3. *Object changing*:

a. A stick becomes a cane, a pool cue, a shoulder carrier, a ladder, a rope, a lover, a toothpick, a hat, a flower, a sword, a guitar, an oar, etc.

b. A hat becomes a roof, a lover, a sex object, a weapon, a pillow, a mirror, a baby, a bandage, etc.

4. *Props*: Use any prop, such as a door, a rug, a wall, etc., to establish a bit of business and a gag. (Watch Keaton films!) You will be introduced to more of this sort of exercise in Comedy Workshop model, Appendix five.

5. *Two people tell a story*: An exercise for two people: one actor stands in front of the other. The actor in front tells a story, but the arms telling the story are those of the actor behind him who has passed his arms under the arms of the person in front. This exercise forces two actors to breathe together, thinking as one!

Part Four: Character Development

1. *Hat game*:

a. An actor chooses a hat and then, defines, in great detail, the physicality of a character, who goes with the hat. The character enters the space (in which there is one plain chair, centre stage, and next to it, on the floor, another hat) and sits down. He must know who he is, where he is, why he is there, and why he sits down. He must sustain his inner monologue so that the audience can know what he is feeling and thinking as he sits there. Gradually the actor leaves his character and returns to a neutral (zero) position in the chair. Only when this is achieved will he pick up the hat on the floor next to the chair. Remaining seated, he will put the new hat on and begin to find the body of the a new character who goes with the hat. Those watching must see the process of the actor's discovery, as the physicality inspired by the new hat takes over his body. When the character is firmly established, the actor rises from the chair and walks out of the space, again, knowing who he is, where he is going, etc.

I have often used this as an audition improvisation. It requires an actor to think clearly and quickly and be responsive to given situations. More importantly, one can quickly determine whether or not the actor is willing to take creative risks while,
at the same time, safely guarding what he knows to be an actors' process. On the contrary, it is equally obvious when an actor relies on physical posing, which results in two-dimensional acting.

b. This time a hat is placed in each of the four corners of the stage space. The actor enters the space at one corner, takes the first hat, makes his decisions, finds the character's physicality and proceeds to walk in a straight line, along the edge of the space towards the next corner of the square.

There he returns to his zero, picks up the second hat and repeats the process of finding a character to go with the hat. In character, he walks along the outside line of the space until he reaches the third hat, where he again repeats the process, etc., until he has tried all four hats and has returned to the place where he began.

2. *Sustaining characters*: This is done while falling, slipping, tripping, and making dramatic use of various acting techniques. The actor walks diagonally across the space, sustaining his well-defined character. Halfway along he trips. The actor's reactions to the trip, the dynamics and inner rhythm, etc. will all be determined by the character and the character's objectives. Despite the technical difficulties, the actor must sustain his character throughout the trip, the recovery from the trip, and until the moment when he exits from the space. The same exercise is repeated with a slip and then with a fall. After he has gone through the process with all three techniques and discovered how the character has related to each mishap, the actor puts all three techniques together into a situation. Walking across the space, he trips, then slips, and finally falls. The actor will be creating a short narrative, and those watching must know a great deal about this character, including what he feels and thinks about falling on his face, etc. The actor is defining the character by finding how he will behave in specific situations.

3. *Animal work*: Defining a character through animal characteristics. (See Part One, Exercise 6.)

4. *Element work*: Defining a character through essential characteristics of the elements: earth, fire, air, water.

5. *Simple actions*: A well-defined character is given a simple action such as a kiss or watching death. After the exercise is completed, discuss with those watching and those doing, the moment before and the moment after the action. Define what happened in the moments preceding the action, e.g., the hesitancy, fear, anticipation, etc., and the moments following the action, e.g., the disappointment, greediness, satisfaction, etc. This is an excellent exercise for illustrating the importance of not getting lost in the act itself.

6. *Physical description*: Apply to a well-defined physicality such words as "frail," "brittle," "oppressed by the heat," "frozen," "melting," "broken," etc. Discuss the results and what the actor has found.

7. *Meetings*: Create a series of meetings of well-defined charac-

ters in specific dramatic moments. The characters, the situations, the objectives must all be clear. (See Part Two, Exercise 5.)

8. *Establishing the essence of an historical character*:

a. A series of frozen images are found that establish the essence of a person's historical role. These images may represent chronological developments in the person's life. They may be images of the most important moments in his life. They may be images that study the essential of that person, etc. In between each image, the actor turns his back to the audience, where he regains his zero, and begins to build the next dramatic moment. As always, he will constantly be making use of an actor's techniques, such as the inner monologue, physical feelings, etc. Then, with a slow pivot, he turns to the audience with the new image intact. This exercise may be helpful, as well, in helping to define the essence of a character in a play.

b. The same exercise as above, but now the actor adds to his series of images one quote from the person's life (or one line from the text of the play) that may aid in establishing the essence of the person's historical role. The actor should choose the best moment to inject the quote, in order to make the desired dramatic impact.

c. Using as a basis the above exercise, create a revolving (pivoting) series of three to five images. Each new image appears much as a statue or series of statues, which rotate on a pedestal. Again, the images can be narrative in character, or they can be a series of parts that explain the whole. The revolving never stops. The actor fades out of one image as he turns his back to the audience and as he returns, the new image emerges.

9. *Developing a character from a painting* (and his role in the dramatic moment):

a. Using actors' techniques such as inner monologues, physical feelings, clear objectives, etc., create the moments preceding the event in the picture. This should provide the action that will take the actor/s into the dramatic moment depicted in the painting. At the moment when the actor/s have actually recreated the picture, they freeze. Then, slowly, they bring the picture back to life, developing the moments that might follow the action of the painting. These moments will, in turn, take the actor out of the painting's frame.

b. After gaining an understanding of the specific situation as depicted in the painting, place the character(s) in another situation, e.g., in a bedroom, in a moment of acute danger, totally exhausted, in a fight, etc.

10. *Building the physicality of a character* (layer by layer):

• The actor begins from his neutral. He begins to create the character's neutral body—defining physically the character's age, physical history, what the person has done with his body throughout his life, his health, work, self-image, class, status, and sex.

• Having established the physical feeling of the character in a neutral state, at a specific point in his history, now place the neutral body in defined outside elements, such as the weather. Is it hot, cold, comfortable?

• Add to this physical feeling the energy level found at the specifically defined dramatic moment, e.g., refreshed, high energy, or exhausted.

• Add to this the "mood" that all the elements making up the dramatic moment have caused in the character.

• Having identified the physical feeling of the character in the specific dramatic situation, the character walks forward, with a clear objective in mind. For example, perhaps he is walking, on a beautiful morning, to a job he hates; or perhaps he is walking, on a very grey day, to a meeting with an ex-lover who he has not seen for five years, etc. The actor must sustain everything he has found throughout this process. If the actor has been successful, all aspects of the character and his life should be clear to the audience.

The breath is the key throughout! This exercise must be preceded by work on each of the physical elements that make up a character's physicality. Work must be done on aging, on physical condition/ health, on energy levels; on the effects of outside elements, such as hot and cold, etc.

11. *Physical Feelings*: The actor moves across the space, in one constant rhythm:

a. From toddler to extreme old age.

b. From extreme hot to extreme cold.

c. From bursting with energy to exhaustion.

d. From total happiness to desperation.

Be careful not to confuse physical feelings that may have similar physical manifestations, but that can be the result of emotionally quite different states, e.g., anger, depression, exhaustion, etc. Instead, explore the differences between them.

Exercises 10 and 11 are probably the most important exercise in the book!

Part Five: Establishing a character within the rehearsal process

1. *Character analysis*: Go through the text, line by line, finding every place where the character is described through his actions, as well as the places where the character is described verbally by the author or other characters. Special note should be made of adverbs used to describe the character, such as "warmly", "reluctantly", "suspiciously", etc.

2. *An autobiography*: Create the character's past life, in great detail.

3. *"A Day in the Life of ..."*: An essay, describing in great detail, a day in the character's life. Always search for clear decisions.

4. *Building the character's physicality*: Work from the neutral, building layer by layer the character's body as described in Part Four Number 10. Take into consideration clothes, self-image, etc.

5. Identifying the essence of the character: Find the minimum necessary to make a clear dramatic statement about the character.

   a. Try one element of make-up, e.g., ruddy or pale; a moustache; a hair style, etc.

   b. Find one prop, e.g., glasses, a stick, a flower, a veil, etc.

   c. Find one line in the text that seems to express the essence of the character.

6. *Sustaining and making use of all that has been learned*: The actors will now use improv techniques to address the difficulties of always sustaining the character's physicality, while establishing clear physical actions, intentions, and objectives. At this point the actor places the physical being he has created into a dramatic moment and gives him a "physical action".

7. *Creating physical situations and discovering physical responses*:
Find the character's physical response to specifically defined situations, e.g., muddy, or perhaps, slippery streets outside, heavy
rain, a heat wave, a snow storm, etc. How does he react when
chilled, or sweaty, when well-scrubbed, or when his clothes have
become filthy, etc.? The actors should work both alone and with
others in this exercise.

a. Try distancing the character from these realities.

b. Ask those who have been watching to close their eyes.
Then ask them which image of the character they have just
seen comes to their mind. They will be identifying the image
that has stayed with them and made the clearest impression.
"Memory is a good poet" (Decroux).

8. *Entrance-Exit*: A character walks into room through a door,
sits down, and then, after a while, leaves the space, through
another door, leading into another room. Everything about the
character must be clear to those watching. What is his age, his
work, his history? Where he is coming from and going to?
What does the space mean to him? What does he want? What
is his dramatic situation at that moment? Finally, why does he
leave the space? The way in which he opens and closes the
door, how he sits down, etc. will provide the clues.

Ask those watching to close their eyes, as they did in the
previous exercise. Then ask them to identify the essential of the
character they have just watched. What is it that they have
retained as the most important characteristics of the character?
Discuss. Why do some images remain with them and others
not?

9. *Scenes of interactions*: Work on specific interactions from the
play, without text, but with detailed inner monologue. This
exercise helps the actor to find a certain clarity, by discarding all
the clutter that can so easily gather around words, as well as by
providing a means to discover and explore details about specific
interactions which words may be serving to cover up, etc.
Please refer to model workshops for more of exercises.

Conclusion

There are hundreds of exercises. The important thing is to know what to look for in an exercise. We must be very clear what it is we need at a given point in the process, be it in the classroom or in rehearsal, and what exactly each exercise serves.

Appendix Three
Mask Workshop

THIS WORKSHOP SCRUTINIZES the effect of the theatrical image, created by the actor, on both the performance space and the audience's perception of what is happening in that space. In the process of creating the visual image of a character, the actor must be aware of and sensitive to how others' perceive his discoveries. The actor, in fulfilling his role as a part of the theatre collective, will need to be simultaneously responsive and responsible to the reactions of both his colleagues and the audience. He must be open and vulnerable to the demands made by others upon his creation.

No where is this process more visible than when working with a mask. A mask does not cover up. In fact with a mask everything is revealed; there is nowhere for the actor to hide. He cannot explain himself with words, nor can he fall back on his tricks or personal charm to lull the audience away from the essence of his role in the situation at hand. With his face hidden by a mask, the actor is naked; if he feigns or fakes a response, it is immediately noticeable. The actor has no choice but to concentrate and listen. As he listens to his inner rhythms and inner monologues (which are in response to the rhythms and impulses of the dramatic moment) he will find himself responding to the dictates of the interactions and relationships evolving about him. Thus enabled to develop the actions and demands of the moment, the actor will find himself being remarkably clear and direct.

Masked, the actor must abandon all excess. Clutter creates misunderstanding as never before. When using a mask, even the most subtle moment becomes visible. The physical image being created becomes so basic and strong that any superfluous "showing" or "demonstrating" will strike both the actor and his colleagues as not only unnecessary, but irrelevant and dishonest.

The actor, at first, may feel an almost desperate need to "explain" to the audience what his character is feeling and thinking. He may find himself actually talking or making grimaces under his mask. Gradually, working within the freedom of his own resources, he begins to feel the joy of trusting himself and opening up physically to the demands of the theatre moment. The mask becomes simply an extension of the character's body. Faced with the need to concentrate and listen so intensely, he finds that it is actually easier to identify and respond to his physical impulses. At such moments, the responses seem just, and the communication becomes vital and clear. When the actor can feel content in his vulnerability, he will be free to let his actor's imagination soar.

THE NEUTRAL MASK

The value of essential movement cannot be more clearly defined than when working with the neutral mask. The unresponsive, inarticulate body seems to hang beneath the mask like a limp rag. When denied excess and explanations, the actors, either watching or doing the exercises, cannot help but realize how easy it is to be misinterpreted or misunderstood. Later, as the actor relaxes and becomes responsive to the demands of the mask, he will remark on how well-defined his objectives have needed to be and how much easier it has been to play creatively within the dramatic moment. The masked, naked body, allows the actor to find the essential of his character and to present his findings in an articulate manner. The actor will find a new freedom under his mask.

It is a wonderful technique to use both in the teaching of actors and in the early stages of rehearsal. All tricks become flagrantly visible and therefore unacceptable. Any lack of physical, emotional, and intellectual clarity simply cannot be tolerated by either the actor or the audience with whom the actor is communicating.

THE EXPRESSIVE OR CHARACTER MASK

The process of creating an expressive mask, especially when masking the whole body, forces the actor to define, in great detail, his character. Led by the mask, he will find the costume or prop to complete the essential image. Working with other characters, masked and/or unmasked, the actor will discover a new freedom, which will help to open up an exploration into the substance of his character and the essence of its relationship to the others.

Again, the actors must look closely at the situation, the space, and their role in relationship to the whole. Familiar improv techniques, as well as the skills used in creating a character, are now applied to this very exacting situation. This work is immensely helpful in developing a character and its interactions with the other masks (characters). The actors will find themselves defining and redefining until the essential emerges. Masks simply permit an extremely honest process of observation and exploration, where discoveries are wonderfully tangible and apparent.

THE EXERCISES

The mask workshop must create an environment whereby the actor is forced to take a clear look at the performance space and how a physical presence fills this space. These exercises, therefore, are designed to help the actor to feel and establish himself in relationship to others through clear theatrical images. They cannot help but reveal to the young actor a great deal about the task of acting.

This work can be used time and again at varying points and phases of an actor's development. Depending on how and when the exercises are utilized, they are, in effect, exercises in concentration, exercises in communication, exercises in space awareness, imagination stimulants, and finally a means into a character.

When working with expressive masks, there is much to be said for the workshop beginning with the actual making of the mask. This requires precise decisions from the very start. The actor is forced to define, in detail, elements that are essential to his character. Depending on time and materials available, there are many ways to go about mask-making (see bibliography). If nothing else is available, the actors can work with makeup to find the essential character as seen in the face.

These exercises are not designed to teach mask as a theatrical form. Mask theatre involves a whole plethora of techniques and skills. However, basic mask techniques will be uncovered as the work unfolds, and it is remarkable how many of the rules of mask work are applicable to most any theatrical presentation.

1. *One Person at a Time*:

a. The mask enters, establishing who he is, and where he is. He establishes a place, a mood, an atmosphere, and an objective. He explores the space and begins an action that will eventually lead him to exit from the space. He must always be clear about who he is in the space and what he wants. Those watching must analyze what they have seen and understood and why.

b. The same exercise as above, only now the character adds a prop.

c. To the above exercise add one piece of set, e.g., a chair.

d. Try using different masks in the same space, working with the same prop and action. This is good for both neutral and expressive mask.

2. *Contradictions within a character—mask versus body*: This exercise explores the outside image and the inner feelings, and the possibilities of making a character's inner conflicts comprehensible to the audience. Find the physicality of the following characters:

Outside:	*Inside*:
criminal	heart of gold
mother/madonna	exhausted, bored mother
energetic YUPPIE	burnt out
generous boss	making millions off his workers

3. *Meetings*:

a. Two characters enter separately into a defined space: a church, a waiting room, a bedroom, a dance hall, a hotel, the moon, the countryside, a photographer's studio, a dance school, amongst a park full of statues, etc. Follow the process established in Exercise 1, allowing now for relationships to develop. Notice the importance of the moment of eye contact.

b. At first, only one of the masks works with a prop. Then allow both masks to have and use a prop.

c. Both masks enter an undefined space at the same moment. They meet and a relationship (perhaps only momentary) is created.

d. Two masks enter from opposite sides of the space, on the diagonal. When they meet, they circle one another. An interaction is established, and they continue on their way, until they have exited.

Note the need for well-motivated actions and for a thorough understanding of the rules for "Entrance-Statement-Exit" exercises. These are good for both neutral and expressive masks.

4. *Masked and unmasked*:

a. An unmasked character creates a space and situation. The masked character then enters. Follow the rules established in former exercises on meetings (See Appendix Two). Analyze carefully. Who dominates? Who controls? Who has status? Why?

b. Allow the unmasked character to speak. What happens?

c. Give props to one or both of the characters.

d. "They're all mad, expect me!" Wonderful Decroux improv that is good for expressive masks.

5. *Conversation in Movement—with mask* (see Appendix Two): This is good for both neutral and expressive masks.

6. *Masked character with outside director*: The masked character defines himself. From outside the space the character is directed by a "director" who will instruct the character where to go and what to do. (Feelings, reactions, decisions, etc. are never given; the only "given" is the action to be taken.) The character must create the situation and justify his actions. The director provides an inner monologue of actions, not feelings. This exercise is good for expressive masks.

7. *Conversation with masked character/s and instruments*:

a. Actors, out of the space, use percussion instruments (or any other instruments that might be available) to carry on a conversation with one or more masks in the space. All the rules for Conversations in Movement must be followed, i.e., one person (or in this case, one musical sound) at a time, etc.

b. One instrument personifies a "character".

c. The entire "orchestra" of sound personifies one "character". Perhaps each sound represents one aspect of the character.

d. Try each sound reflecting a "character". Work in establishing several sound/characters, but only one masked character.

e. The instruments take on the role of the "director" as in Exercise 5, this time creating an inner monologue of feelings, which are in response to the masked character's actions. This will, in turn, lead the mask on to new actions.

f. The instruments create an atmosphere for a Conversation in Movement between several masks. Be aware of the give and take, i.e., when the atmosphere dictates the action, and when the action dictates the atmosphere. This exercise is good for expressive masks.

8. *Sustaining the situation when the mask is removed*: Follow the rules of Exercises 1, 2, and 4, to create situations, interactions, relationships, etc. Then, removing the masks, carefully sustain and develop all that has been created.

9. *Inner Monologue Exercises*:

a. Develop theatrically, the following inner monologue: "I see. I'm interested. I'm fearful. It's funny. No, it's horrible. It's gone. I want that. No, I'd rather have that. What's that I see coming? It's coming closer. It's stepping over me! Disappeared! Wasn't anything. Not really!"

b. Try developing an inner monologue for the following situation: Enter. See something. Want it. Examine it. It's funny. No, it's slimy. It disappears. Search for it and find two instead. Confusion! Which one is wanted? Inner conflict!

c. See an object. Take it. It reminds the character of something else: Look at the object and have an idea.

d. Take something others aren't to see.

Conclusion

It is hoped that, these exercises will lead to situations and ideas where mask work can be further used to develop the actors' sensitivity to, and use of physical presence in, the dramatic situation. As always, this work is presented here as a point of departure.

In Appendix Two many exercises are indicated as being very useful when carried out with masks.

Appendix Four
Ensemble Acting Workshop: Group Movement as an Actor's Technique

THIS WORKSHOP INTRODUCES the concept of actors working closely together to create images of groupings (the masses, or crowds, etc.) that appear to have one entity or identity, but from which other groups or individuals can emerge. The workshop's exercises explore the theatrical use of such images to create the many-faceted thoughts of an individual (as in Greek chorus) or images where the group or mob is used to make clear statements on social entities or interactions. "The groupings and movement of the characters has to narrate the story, which is a chain of incidents (actions), and this is the actor's sole task." (Brecht,B., in *Brecht on Theatre*, ed. John Willett, New York: Hill and Wang, 1964), p.213.

The use of mass movement to express, for example, a sense of dramatic historical process, or struggles and conflicts (be they internal or external) can be very successful. The workshop looks at how the mass/chorus can become one common body, one being, with one inner rhythm, one heart (or centre) so to speak. It is a study on how actors can think, act and react together, as one. Such work allows both the subtlest or most dynamic of actions to be expressed with theatrical clarity. A whole gamut of powerful emotional images can emerge. The merest flicker of a hand in the crowd or a sigh at a meeting, for example, can command a formidable dramatic strength, as can, indeed, the overpowering rhythm of a mob on the march.

The actors must keep in mind that masses are groups of individuals, who, when they are together and share something in common, make up a crowd. Five people breathing together, sharing the same centre, can become a crowd. In fact, five people can become a very forceful mass, depending on the elements surrounding the situation. The individuals must find what it is they share in common, which makes them a unit. If they lose it, they will no longer be a crowd. A break in the essence they share will cause a strong dramatic statement, a change of focus, a rupture.

The rules for communicating a clear, credible action are the same, whether it be for a common body of many actors or one individual actor. Every movement must have its motivation or physical action, dictated by the objectives of the dramatic moment. Clear decisions must be made. Movement will always begin from the inside, in response to internal or external stimuli. Breath remains the clear indicator of emotion; eyes remain the clear interpreter of thought. Each movement is an offer or response; it's meaning clear only when economical in execution. It is through a control of the level of tension that an actor is able to create clear interactions and direct the audience's focus. Through inner rhythm, emotional statements are made. Rhythm, expressed through breath, is like a sign of life and gives life to the dramatic moment. And through design, the image is created, which, in turn, defines the interactions and relationships.

A crowd breaths as one. Those who make up the crowd do not necessarily move together. What makes them a unit is that they share the same centre. Five people can create a crowd, but if one person breaks the rhythm, an individual in the crowd has been created, and the focus has changed.

An interesting study is to look at the individual within the mass. Dialogue between the two will be as between two actors. Such interactions—between the individuals who make up the group, between an individual and the group, or between the groups themselves—are dramatically explicit. The emotional rhythm of the whole is felt, as well as the individual's rhythm within the whole. The roles of "the leader" and of "the outsider" are, for example, two powerful elements affecting the whole. Such work is an extremely good vehicle for studying the use of focus, as well as status and how and why it is acquired.The moment of drama is when the eyes meet.

Neutral masks are an excellent resource for this work, as they emphasize the use of movement as the sole reflecter of thought and feeling. They permit no excess. Every sigh or glance cannot help but be visible and meaningful. The actor must be in control of every statement that is being made.

THE EXERCISES

In order to establish and develop these ideas, it is necessary to introduce the techniques that are the basis of the physical actor's language and to provide a sense of how these techniques can be used to make clear dramatic statements. The exercises serve as an introduction to a way of thinking and working in theatre. Much of the process may become clear only towards the end of the work-shop. It is, however, exactly this sense of process that must be diligently followed through to its conclusion. Such physical work requires the actors to plunge into the work and then carefully analyze what has taken place. The ability to listen intently and respond physically (not verbally) is a skill to be learned. So is group concentration—perhaps the most difficult task demanded by this work-shop.

Part One: The Warm- Up

The warm-up must include: *body work* (as in Exercises 1,3,4,); *space awareness work*—where the actor must function with others in a changing space, always aware of the design being created (as in Exercises 2, 5, 6, 7, 8, 9, and 10); *work on interactions*—where the actors are concentrating on their mutual inter-dependence in creating interactions and relationships (as in Exercises 2, 3, 5, 6, 7, 8, and 9); *the use of isolated movement,* (esp.Exercises 1, 4, and 9) and finally *work on intensity*—levels of tension (Exercises 2, 4, and 5); *on rhythm*—explosive/lyrical, rapid/slow, etc., noticing the change of rhythm dictated by inner or outer stimuli (Exercises 1,2,4,8,9,19, and 11) and *on design*—what the body is doing in relationship to the space and others in the space (Exercises 1, 2, 4, 5, 6, 7, and 11).

1. *Follow the leader* * : An exercise in imitating movement with great attention to detail, all the while, walking in a circle.

2. *Walking the lines of the space* * : An exercise for awareness of self and others in the space.

a. Block one another, creating an obstacle course.

b. While running, change the rhythm, as directed by the outsider.

c. Create a magnetic field.

d. Create a pattern of ten steps forward and repeat it, moving backwards.

e. As above, only now work with the eyes closed.

f. Create relationships with one other in the space and then continue their development until they both exit. It is necessary to follow the rules of the exercise at all times (never breaking the rhythm, never stopping, or speaking, or moving off the horizontal and vertical lines, etc.). When finished, discuss what each actor understood to be his partner's objective. What did each want from the other, etc.? How much of this was clear to those watching?

3. *Figure Eight* * : At first, try the figure walking and then speed it up to a run.

4. *Gentle stretches of total body* * : Use the weight and support of a partner.

5. *Individual Warm-Up in Group* * : Pay special attention to: a) the joints, b) listening to and following the impulse of a movement, c) taking a movement to its conclusion, d) the intensity, rhythm, and design of a movement, creating resistance in space.

6. *Tangle* *

7. *Points of balance* * : Working in groups of three (and then five), create human structures, following a dictated number of points of balance.

8. *Minimum points of balance* *

9. *Walking the quadrate* *

10. *Domino movement in groups*: A group of five to ten actors place themselves close together in a line. In quick succession

(one person following the impulse of another), a movement repeats itself, moving up and down the line. The movement and the movement's rhythm must always be the same. Try, at first, simple movements, such as a head turning, an arm moving, the eyes glancing to the side, legs lifting, the total body inclining, etc. It is as if one movement actually causes the same movement in the next person.

a. Try in differing rhythms.

b. Try changing directions, etc.

c. Try with eiffel towers, pivots, head movements, legs crossing, etc.

d. Try with each group creating a pattern.

e. Try combinations of two or more movements, e.g., the head rotates and then total inclines, etc.

11. *Explosive and lyrical movement* * : Constantly moving from the floor to a maximum height, the actor explores explosive (angular) and lyrical (round, curved) movement, as dictated by the clap of hands from an outsider.

12. *Trust exercises* *

Not all of these exercises must be done at each session. However, one must always begin with group warm-ups, i.e., Exercises 1, 2, 3, and 8, and then body warm-ups, i.e., Exercises 4 and 5).

*Refer to descriptions of these exercises in Appendices One and Two.

Part Two: Introduction to Ensemble Acting

These exercises include all the basic elements of physical acting: *breath and inner rhythm*—movement begins from the inside and the body must be responsive to this "motor" or beginning of a movement; *immobility*—the use and dramatic power of stillness when addressing the questions of "weight" and "presence" and "living immobility"; *diction-in-movement*—every movement has a dramatic value and, like words, must be clear, precise, and void of excess; *motivation*—one never moves without a reason; *interaction based on physical response*—a study of cause and effect, such as resonance from a shock; *conversation-in-movement*—listening and responding (emphasizing the idea of the unit); *moment of encounter*—meetings, emphasizing the differing levels of contact, i.e., eye contact, actual physical touch, the hesitant gesture, etc., as well as power and status and their reversal; *inner monologue; focus*—bringing the audience's attention to different moments; "all is not equal".

1. *The machine* *

2. *Shock/Resonance* * : An exercise that looks at where an impulse begins and how it differs with an internal and external motor of a movement, i.e., striking out or being struck, etc. Emphasis must be placed on the following of a movement through to its conclusion.

3. *Levels of Tension* * : "Continued intense rhythm gives the feeling of a mob" (Decroux).

"Intensity replaces time" (Decroux). Intensity is measured by rhythm the length of time spent at each level of intensity.

a. Moving through space, observe the changes in the level of tension due to the changes in the dramatic situation. Notice the changes in physicality as intensity increases or decreases. Notice where the focus is and how it changes. At first, work individually, moving through space in a straight line. Pay special attention to the inner monologue.

b. Use the exercise where two people meet: they approach each other on the oblique, meet and then exit, together or separately. When two people with clearly defined inner dramas meet, a new level of tension will result.

c. Lecoq's Seven Levels of Tension

(1) baby/drunk

(2) relaxed/laid back

(3) neutral

(4) light/sigh/air/float

(5) fire/explosive

(6) melodrama

(7) complete tension/immobility

d. Two groups, working as a unit, approach each other. Notice the changes in intensity, depending on the situation and the relationship that emerge.

4. *Passage to Opposites* * :

a. Moving through the space in a straight line, the actor goes from one physical and emotional state of being to its opposite, e.g., a feeling of well-being to one of anger; from rich to poor (the struggle here is in maintaining one's dignity); from altruism to egoism, etc. Always try to reverse the exercise and return to the situation in which one began. Pay special attention to process, always using inner monologue. It is a very useful practice, at first, to speak aloud the inner monologue aloud.

b. Try the same exercise as above, only this time remaining in place.

c. Create a total change in status, e.g., clerk to company director, soldier to general; petty thief to gang leader; pupil to teacher, etc. Always move through the space at the same rhythm and along the same line. The actor must finish the metamorphosis at the same moment he arrives at the end of the space. At this point, sustaining all that he has found, he turns and reverses the process, returning to his original place and situation, i.e., as a clerk, etc.

d. Try the above states of being. However, this time, there are two groups in the well-defined roles. Each group begins from an opposite point; their meeting will cause a reversal of roles.

5. *Puppet* * : Actors pull one another on invisible strings. Not only will they be creating harmonious movement, but the interaction will be reflected as well in the rhythm of the movement. Breath is the leading element that will allow the actors to feel one another's presence through space.

a. Try imagining the string attached to the chest, to the back, to the head, etc.

b. Try the imaginary strings attached to the fingers of both parties.

6. *Conversations in Movement* * : Every movement has its' dramatic value. All excess must be totally avoided. Special attention must be given to unit work and, again, to the inner monologue. This is very much a study in "living immobility." Never play the "petit personnage." Always remember, not all is equal—avoid monotone movement!

a. Work with one piece of set, e.g., a chair, a screen, etc.

b. Try three different characters working with the same object.

c. With the actors playing animals, attach to each creature a word, e.g., cat/slinky, squirrel/hesitancy, dog/bouncy, bull/power, etc. Later, keep the word and attach it to a character.

7. *Tableaux* * : These are excellent exercises in preparation for the work at the end of the workshop, when the actors must "create a dramatic moment."

*Refer to descriptions of these exercises in Appendices One and Two.

Part Three: Group Movement

These exercises are designed to allow actors, in groups of five to seven people, to learn to work together as a unit. The work involves learning to feel physically as one: breathing together, moving together, sharing as a unit, the same intensity, rhythm, design. Breath and physical contact are used, for example, to develop a sensitivity to each other's presence. One becomes aware, not only of the space in relationship to one's own body, but also gains a perception of that space from the point of view of the crowd. The unit becomes free to move in all directions: up, down, forward, backwards, sideways, etc., and to change these directions. The focus, tension, rhythm, etc. of the mass can also change. The unit walks, runs, shrinks, expands. The weight and power of stillness and inaction can be explored. A change in direction of the mass can be caused by a) each individual within the unit turning on the same breath (for example, 180 degrees), or b) by the whole unit in one breath changing its direction by pivoting about itself.

At first, the actors will designate a "leader" and later this role will change as the actors take over this responsibility from each other. The leader is the heart and mind of the unit. He is, in fact, the "motor of the movement." When the groups succeed in truly feeling "as one," two or more groups can begin to work together to create interactions, and relationships. Status can be looked at. The role of the "outsider" can be developed. Roles change. The leader becomes a follower, the frightened become confident, etc. Individuals can emerge from the group and then return to the mass. The actors must be extremely sensitive to their colleagues—noting every change in breath, every impulse. They must listen to and receive every emotional and intellectual signal being expressed.

As always, it is important for those observing the work to analyze what they see and what they understand by the images created in the dramatic space.

1. *Forming Groups*:

a. Experiment in how groups can be formed best. How can all the actors be aware of all their colleagues? How, when an actor is in the back of a group, can he know what is happening in the front? How best can the impulses run through the group and be sensed by everyone? On what is the communication based? How close, physically, do the actors need to be to one another?

b. Have everyone touch shoulders, and then try having everyone touching heads. Try having everyone look in the same direction. Then try forming a clump—everyone touching but facing in many directions and in many different physical positions perhaps resting most of one's weight on one's nearest colleague. Breathe together.

c. In forming the above positions, allow the actors to give their weight to one another. Notice that it is necessary for the actors to have weight on both feet, if any kind of change in the balance structure or movement through space is attempted.

2. *Movement of the Groupings*:

a. Breathe together. Find a common rhythm and intensity.

b. Move within this breath. At first, the group goes up on tip toe and then down to deep plié. Try swaying together, side to the side, and forwards and backwards (first while standing solidly, and then when up on tip toe or deep in plié). Try swaying the total mass, which will involve inclinations of the total in all directions, and then only from the waist. Try moving just the heads -rotating and inclining them, etc. Allow the eye focus of the group to fix in various directions. The group will notice the importance of breathing together and following the breath's impulse.

c. In groups, try to create different rhythms, e.g., forcefully moving forward, then holding back. Try repetitive rhythms like those in nature (waves, wind, etc.).

d. Designate a leader who will be responsible for leading the group. As his objectives change, so will his directions. The group must follow him, always breathing as one, echoing his intensities, rhythms, his switch in focus, the directions in which the action goes, his inner monologue, etc. He is the core of the group, and when he is successful, his signals will be easy to follow and develop. If he is unclear about "what he wants," it will also be unclear to all the other actors, and all communication will break down. Those further away from the leader are dependent upon the other actors to transmit what is happening. The actor's senses will need to be very acute; everyone is dependent on and responsible to everyone else.

e. Allow the role of the leader to change hands. One actor takes over from another. The new leader will "interrupt" the process of the other. There will be a change in direction, a change in rhythm, a change in objective. It is very important that the new leader is extremely clear. Everyone in the unit must feel and be made aware of his intentions. The changeover is instantaneous, and there can be no doubt in anyone's mind as to who is now in charge. The group must work together, aware of each colleague. The need to give and take has never been more clear.

f. The group moves together under the leadership of the leader; he makes the decisions, and takes the actions, based on dramatic need, and the whole moves with him. Special attention must be paid to the cause of the action. The motor of the movement must be the same for every part of the whole, and not just for the leader. If a movement is the result of an emotional pain, or in response to a decision to retreat, it must be clear. As the unit moves, the situation will develop. The objectives of the unit must be clear to everyone, both those doing and those observing.

g. Switch leaders again and again. One person takes over from another. The signals must be very clear, so that they are felt by everyone in the unit.

h. Make use of the single, small, individual movement. Notice how one small movement, emerging from the mass, can take on more dramatic importance than the whole group tumbling from a great height. Notice its power and how a tilted head, or a hand, or even a finger can change the entire dramatic situation.

3. *Meetings of groups*: Use various exercises for meetings as described in the Appendix Three (The Mask Workshop), and Appendix Two. However, the meetings now are of groups. Try the exercises with both large and small groups and with a combination of the two. The reason for any change, i.e., in status, a reversal of direction, etc., must be clear to those watching.

a. Try having several groups working in the space at one time, so that complex interactions and relationships can develop.

b. Experiment with the dynamics of push-pull.

c. Experiment with the power of eye contact.

d. Try status changes in groups, e.g., between cats and dogs, men and women, leader and follower, soldier and general, etc.

e. Each group decides on a word which describes the state of being of the group. As the groups meet, there is a reversal in their states of being; e.g., from altruism to egoism, from anger to kindness, from exhaustion to high energy, etc.

f. Try meetings of groups that evoke animal characteristics, e.g., swans, eagles, fish, cocks, octopi, horses, monkeys, snails, sharks, etc. Find the animals' rhythms, and notice how the essence of the animal behaves in meetings with other animals.

g. Try meetings of a group with an outsider. Try using animals again, i.e., a pack of dogs and a cat, etc. At first, the groups are the animals and then they develop into characters with the animal characteristics

h. Try other exercises exploring the relationship between the mass and individuals, e.g., one tries to remain unseen by the mass, or "All I want is to be left alone", etc.

Part Four: Creating a Dramatic Moment

Working in groups of eight to twelve actors, decide on a specific atmosphere, e.g., a storm at sea, a shipwreck, the January sales, a political or ideological demonstration, a prison yard, an execution, the peace in a small town before a storm, a specific square or park, etc. Try scenes of struggle, of marching, and of destruction. Try tragic scenes and comic scenes. Never play generalities. No two mob scenes, for example, are ever the same.

Make clear decisions concerning what the mass wants in the space. What is the relationship of individuals to the mass? Who or what is the mass? Who are the individuals within the mass? What is the primary objective of the mass? How does this differ from those of the individuals?

Decide on the first image—the beginning of the dramatic moment. Be clear about what it is the group is trying to communicate. Begin to let the picture move. Do not talk. Using the various techniques and methods central to the previous exercises (e.g., the units, the roles of the individuals who make up the unit, the interaction of different groupings, the joining and breaking away from groupings, etc.), allow the situation to develop. Avoid, at all cost, pantomiming and demonstrating. Allow the dramatic moment to evolve organically, keeping in mind the primary objective. At first find the rhythm of the whole. Moving in slow motion, bring the situation to life, letting the parts of the whole emerge.

When the final statement is reached, freeze it. Every relationship between the groups and individuals in the groups should be visible and clear. Remark how the relations have changed (or not) in comparison to the first frozen image. Bring the "piece" to its conclusion. Exit with the primary objective still clear.

Show to the other groups. Discuss what has been seen and understood. Define the dramatic significance. Go back together to rework. Make new decisions based on the discussions. Rework the whole "piece" and re-show. With one's colleagues, analyze the "problems" yet again. Go back to rework, and then show for the final time.

Appendix Five

Comedy Workshop: An Approach to Comic Acting

THIS WORKSHOP HAS BEEN DEVISED as an approach to
clowning and the creating of comic characters. It is concerned with
helping the actor to understand how he can find and explore the
comic in theatrical situations. The study of comic techniques and the
clown is, in itself, long and demanding, requiring the mastery of a
great many theatrical skills. It is hoped that students will understand this workshop as a stepping off point from which courses in
commedia, clowning and archetypical characters should follow.

Such an introduction to comedy will require the actor to look
very closely at specific problems of physical acting. The actor will
need to use his acting skills and physical techniques in new ways, in
order to create the comic moment. The work emphasizes, more than
ever, the actor's need for economic movement and precision.

It is necessary for the actors to constantly analyze the work that
they and their colleagues produce. They will need to ask why a piece
of work has been clear and therefore "successful" and likewise, why
not. What, for example, makes something funny, and to whom?

It is very important to take the time to repeat the comic
moments being created. The work must be presented, thoroughly
discussed, re-rehearsed, and presented again. This process must

happen at least three times. In this way, problems can be ironed out "on the floor" and not merely identified and abandoned.

The actors will need to be looking at and thinking about a variety of things. Obviously, questions concerning why and when something is amusing will become very pertinent. Which images bring smiles to which faces? Is there such a thing as universal humor? If not, how is it socially and culturally defined? Certainly the theatrical use of what is socially outside of the norm, in order to distance that norm, will be crucial to the work.

There are many basic principles that the actor must follow. He must remember that it is the situation that is funny and that he, therefore, must not try to be funny. He must play the situation. The clown, Lecoq will tell you, takes himself very seriously, and tries so hard.

The comic actor has chosen comedy as the best means to communicate his ideas. He will find the "laugh" in much the same way he finds any dramatic situation. Initially, he must set up a situation, which then proceeds to take him by surprise. He must not plan it. He must not wait for something to happen. Rather, he must find these moments, put his finger on them, and play them.

What is often seen as a comic action is not, in itself, funny. Eating a shoe or slipping on a banana peel is comic only within the dramatic context. The actor chooses to bring out the comic or tragic elements in the situation. Often, when presented with comedy, the audience discovers tragedy. Such is the beauty of comedy.

The actor's role is not unlike the film editor's. His task is to present the material, as he chooses, in order to focus the audience. The audience sees the situation through the character and the character's actions, and it is the actor who will make the moment appear absurd or funny or tragic. The comic actor would do well to keep in mind Charlie Chaplin's dictum. "What appears to be sane is really insane" Rolfe, B., *Mimes on Miming*, (London, Millington, 1981), p.118. The actor must play the character straight, and it is up to the audience to react with laughter. Laughter comes for many reasons. The comic actor touches his audience in many ways. No where is this more apparent than in the films of Charlie Chaplin.

Incompatible elements often bring about comedy. The actor must find them, and find the image to exploit and emphasize the contradiction. Often the comic actor will use a fleeting glance as a technique to focus the audience, achieving comedy through frequent repetition of these moments.

Decroux was fond of reminding us that comedy was "a change in direction." He was speaking about the role of the unexpected; about catching the audience unawares. If a moment is not to be anticipated by the audience, the actor must carry out his action with absolute conviction. "The man who doesn't believe isn't funny" (Decroux). He must also have precision and control of his movements; he must have the ability to change speed, to remain immobile, or to "stop on a dime."

The workshop begins by learning to create caricatures. This, I understand to be the physical paring down of a character in order to reveal and emphasize specific characteristics. The actor is, in fact, discovering the comic essence of his character. Through this process the actor will aim to discover and present essential characteristics of relationships and social situations through a comic language.

At the same time, the actor must be learning the tools of the comic's trade: the stock comedy routines and gags. Some people will tell you that every comic gag is a variation on eight themes; for others the magic number seems to be twelve. But whether the clown is chasing a flea in his trousers, or bumping into a door, or is a victim of mistaken identity, the gag must not be separated from the dramatic situation. The actor must nurture his comic imagination by making use of the gag. Falling on one's face is only funny in context of character and situation.

When the clown trips, slips, or falls, we are concerned for him and what the action means to him. The fall, in itself, is meaningless. It must reveal something about the character: who is he and where is he going? The action will have a connotation for the audience outside the character, but the actor must be inside the character. The falls, the bumps, the tumbles in a bit of slapstick are all an expression of the characters' relationships to each other and to the situation.

Comic timing is a skill, to be learned. There are exercises to help the actor develop this elusive quality. The exercises will include work on non-anticipation, on a developed sense of the moment, and, most important, never too much or too little.

As always, the physical skills must serve the dramatic moment. That is why they must be integrated into the acting training. The actor must be able to maintain credibility of pain when his toe is stepped on, even if he is hopping about on one leg, cuddling the injured toe like a baby. Two dimensional characters, with two dimensional feelings, leave the actor no where to go and no way to develop the situation. Laughter leaves the audience open. It is a useful theatre element, necessary to all actors.

Part One: The Caricature

1. *Defining the comic character*: This exercise is concerned with discovering and emphasizing the most essential characteristics of a character. By taking away the superfluous, the actor can define all that is central to the character's being. Through exaggerating the comic essence of a character, the comic in human situations can unfold.

a. At first the actors work with their personal physicality, (they often find this very embarrassing and don't like it!). The group is asked to walk about the space. They are asked to identify and analyze the rhythm of their walk. They are asked to discover how they hold their weight and which part of their body seems to lead. They are asked to be conscious of the independence or interrelationship of the appendages of their body (their arms, legs, head, etc.) to their torso. How is the head carried? How does the whole body move in the space? What is the role of the knees, of the ankles, of the feet?

They are asked to emphasize the most important or notable characteristics of their walk, and then to make these tendencies larger (dropping, at the same time, parts of their physicality that seem irrelevant). A hand or arm may swing more widely. A natural tendency to carry the weight backwards will be emphasized by placing the weight as far back as possible. By working in this way, the actor will bring focus to those qualities that are essential to his physicality or that of his character. Comedy must be based in reality. We build the caricature by enlarging the natural and then taking it to (what may initially feel like) absurd lengths. In doing so, we find the comic in a character.

b. After the actors have worked on and presented a physical caricature of themselves, they are asked to develop a caricature of a character they know well—one whose physicality they have analyzed and with which they are familiar. They will repeat the process they have just done on themselves, but with this new body.

2. *Presenting the Caricature*: Entrance-statement-exit. The actor is asked to find, through an image and situation, a clear dramatic statement that will present the essence of the character he has developed.

a. The actor must find a way to bring the character into the performing space and to present him to the audience. He will be looking for the minimal, uncluttered image and gesture, which will permit the audience to understand a great deal about the character: who he is, where he is, and with what motivations and feelings he has entered the space.

He will then try to develop an action that will clarify the character and his objective—what he wants from his situation (and perhaps even from life). He will be making a clear theatrical statement. At one point, he must, in some way, directly acknowledge or even involve the audience: a look, a glance, a response, a rejection of the audience's presence, etc.

With this accomplished, the character will find a need to leave the space. The exit must be as clear as the entrance: a development of who he is, and what he wants to gain by leaving his current situation.

b. Take two of the caricatures and repeat the same process. They enter separately into an undefined space and develop an articulate comic moment. They must define who they are, and what they expect and want from one another. Separately or together, they involve the audience; and separately or together, they will exit.

This exercise requires real collectivity amongst the actors. As before, the work should be developed, presented, discussed, reworked, re-presented, rediscussed, reworked, and finally presented for a third time.

Part Two: Physical Skills for the Comic Actor

1. *Tumbling Skills*:

    a. Try rolls.

    b. Try dives (over objects, over people, under people, etc.).

    c. Try falls (on the face, backwards, to the side, group falls backwards, etc.).

    d. Try pyramids (including kneeling, sitting and standing on shoulders, etc.).

    e. Try cartwheels.

    f. Try pinwheels (double rolls).

    g. Try leap frog.

    h. Try jumping on backs.

    i. Try the caterpillar (lines of people fall backwards, eventually rolling over on top of each other and exit).

    j. Try throwing people over your back.

2. *Mime Skills*:

    a. Establish a space, e.g., distance, height, walls, etc.

    b. Establish illusionary, inanimate objects, e.g., ropes, balls, birds, flowers, clothing, etc. Then give them a dramatic value, such as clothing that is too skimpy or a tug-of-war with a rope, etc.

    c. Establish and define an environment, where one finds, for example, ice or puddles, where it is hot or cold, where there are people passing, or birds and other little animals, etc.

    d. Establish illusionary scenery, e.g., doors, windows, etc.

    e. Create situations where objects affect the subject, e.g., flower pot falls on one's head, etc. Then turn the subject around: Create a situation where the subject affects an object, e.g., when an object is handled, it changes it's shape and/or dramatic value, etc. Try a variety of objects.

    f. Try techniques of sliding, tripping, pushing and pulling, being pushed and being pulled, etc.*

    g. Explore being hit or moved by invisible objects, e.g., something falls on the head or into the eyes; the wind blows you off your feet, etc.

3. *Preparatory Skills in Controlling the Comic Space*:

a. Walk (and later run) in crowded space. All the actors must stop abruptly ("on a dime") at a signal given by an outsider. They must never bump into one another and must work in absolute quiet.

b. Repeat the above exercise, only this time, walk or run backwards.

c. In a given amount of time a group of actors attempt to touch all the walls of the space and return to the exact spot where they began the exercise. The amount of time they have to do this will depend on the outsider, who will, for example, count to ten, etc., depending on the size of the space. They must work in absolute quiet and never touch one another. Repeat until everyone gets it right.

d. Walk or run the lines of space with obstacles. *

4. Props: Props can be used to introduce a character and then, with use, become the symbol of his essence. We have only to think of Chaplin's cane, Marceau's flower, Lloyd's glasses, Popov's hat, etc., to understand the immense possibilities a prop opens up to the comic actor. A cane for one character will have a different raison d'etre for another.

Props are also helpful in finding the comic possibilities of the dramatic situation at hand. Rugs, doors, ladders, etc., can be useful to the comic actor when establishing who he is in relationship to the space and to others in the space, e.g., hiding under a rug and being sat upon or always leaving through a door at the moment when others enter, etc.

And, as Lecoq points out, a red nose can't play tragedy.

a. Change the value and meaning of props: * E.g., *a stick* becomes a cane, a toothpick, a broom, a lover, a flower, a baby, a sword, a snooker cue, a screen behind which to hide, a shoulder carrier, a ladder, a reoccurring obstacle, etc.; a hat becomes a baby, a dance partner, a sex object, a steering wheel, a weapon or shield, a pillow, a blanket, a symbol of status, a pet dog, etc.; a rug, a book, a box...almost anything at hand can be tried.

b. Discover how many ways one can come in and out of a door.

c. Explore all possibilities for hiding in the space, using existing props or scenery.

* refer to Appendices One and Two for more about these exercises.

5. *Creating Comic Images*:

a. Take one's comic character on an obstacle walk: out through a door, over an icy patch, over a rocky path, over a creek or a mud puddle, into a wall, etc. At one point, something falls on his head, and, at another, he gets lost in a crowd. The actors use the same series of obstacles (but in any order) and try to make sense of the character and the situation.

b. Beginning in a frozen image, explore all the possibilities this physical position allows and create a comic but plausible series of events. For example, the actor begins by balancing on one leg, and then finds a series actions and situations (one leading into the other) that creates a comic moment. Perhaps he begins by tying his shoelace, or smelling the shoe after having stepped in something rather awful, or avoiding falling into a pit, or preparing to kick a dog, etc. From there, let it develop—always on one leg! At first try the exercise individually, and then work with two actors, developing an interaction that comes out of their initial positions.

c. Try meetings between two characters. Each enters the space individually and with a minimum of movement (e.g., a walk, or the specific use of a prop, etc.) establishes who he is. When the actors meet, their objective is to secure status over the other. Let the situation develop. Each action or image in which each finds himself should be heightened. Take the physicalization of the moment to the absurd; e.g., if, in a naturalistic situation, the actor would grab the other from behind, now he will climb on his back!

d. Establish a character, a mood, an atmosphere, or a place and then, speeding up all natural movement, explore the situation.

e. Try prop exchanges. The actors make clear entrances (as in the last exercise), only this time each has a prop. The principle motivation for each actor is that he wants the other's prop. Let the situation develop until they both exit. The actors must be very clear as to why they wanted the prop. Later on, break down the actions that were developed and discuss. This will reveal whether the actions did indeed have a purpose or not! Was there a tendency to play the gag without an action?

Afterwards, there must be discussion on how the action "felt" and how believable impulses and physical feelings can be sustained in such absurd context.

6. *Comic routines, comic bits, lazzi:* There are many books containing comic and clowning routines, and so, I will offer only a few of my favorites. The important thing to remember is that the situation is only funny if the character/s (i.e.,the innocent victim, the villain, the hapless soul, always in trouble, etc.), are properly distanced and then focussed upon.

a. Try a chase. The relationship between the chased and chaser must be clear before the chase begins. A cat and dog chase will be dramatically different from a cat and mouse chase, which is, again, totally different in character and rhythm from a cat stalking and chasing a bird. A chase, like anything else in the theatre space must be concrete and tangible. The classic chase between authority and deviant will find its comedy depending on the social context that the actors are addressing, i.e., the cop and the crook is substantially different from CIA/revolutionary, teacher/truant, boss/idle worker, the Giant/Jack, etc. The chase is not an idea in itself, but the essence of an interaction.

b. Try comedy "bits" based on commedia lazzi:

(1) sneaking up on someone

(2) stealing kisses

(3) pulling out surprising things from pockets: e.g., a pork chop or wilted flower, etc.

(4) piggy backs

(5) bumps

(6) blows

(7) tears

(8) disguises—change of class, gender, etc.

(9) hiding: hiding in sack and then being beaten or carried away; hiding under table and at an appropriate moment the table walks away, etc.

(10) acrobatic feats: boxing with feet; tripping over one another; backing into one another, etc.

(11) chases

(12) domestic troubles

(13) lover's troubles

(14) eating: hunger, greed, etc.

Conclusion

The work of the comic actor is, "...this transforming the little every-day annoyances...into some strange and terrific thing", Grock in B. Rolfe, *Mimes on Miming* (London: Millington, 1981), p.115.

Commedia teaches us that we must never lose sight of the human quality that brings every "comic bit" to life. The classic lazzo of a chair being pulled out from beneath someone about to sit down is only as good as the actor doing it. How do the characters involved feel about it? This question will be the actor's starting point for exploration. Real feelings: love, hunger, envy, etc., are at the basis of all action.

Lecoq talks about clowning as one level of theatre rather than as a theatre style. The clown, he says, is in a state of naïveté, and the drama is in holding onto the humanity that the innocent in trouble brings to us. The clown is always trying to do something he knows he can do. Remember how Grock could always play his music so well from behind the screen but who always failed in front of the audience? Lecoq reminds us that clowning is about failing: moving the piano instead of the stool, or falling on one's bottom while dancing. Here is one of his exercises that particularly explores these ideas:

The actor comes on stage triumphantly, to take his bows and receive his applause. But he messes it up. He cannot accept that he is a "flop." He has come on thinking that he is the best in the world and halfway through, realizes he is a "flop." It is his inability to accept this state of affairs that makes him tragic.

Selected
Reading List

Barba, Eugenio. *Beyond the Floating Islands*. New York: PAJ Publications, 1986.

Barrault, Jean-Louis. *Reflections on the Theatre*. London: Rockliff, 1951.

———. *The Theatre of Jean-Louis Barrault*. London: Barrie and Rockliff, 1961.

———. *Memories of Tomorrow*. London: Thames and Hudson, 1974.

Boal, Augusto. *Theatre of the Opressed*. London: Pluto Press, 1979.

Braun, Edward. *Meyerhold on Theatre*. London: Methuen, 1991.

———. *The Theatre of Meyerhold: Revolution on the Modern Stage*. London: Methuen, 1986.

———. *The Director and the Stage: From Naturalism to Grotowski*. London: Methuen, 1987.

Brook, Peter. *The Empty Space*. New York: Avon Books, 1969.

———. *The Shifting Point*. London: Methuen, 1988.

Bruder, Melissa, et al. *A Practical Handbook for the Actor.*
New York: Vintage Books, 1986.

Craig, Gordon. *The Art of the Theatre.* New York: Theatre Arts
Books, 1956.

Decroux, Etienne. *Paroles sur le mime.* Paris: Gallimard, 1963.

——. *Words on Mime.* Claremont, California: Mime Journal, 1985.

Felner, Mira. *Apostles of Silence: The Modern Frence Mimes.*
Cranbury, New Jersey: Associated University Presses, 1985.

Fo, Dario. *The Tricks of the Trade.* London: Methuen, 1991.

Grotowski, Jerzy. *Towards a Poor Theatre.* London: Methuen,
1992.

Huston, Hollis. *The Actor's Instrument: Body Theory on Stage.*
Ann Arbor, Michigan: The University of Michigan Press,
1992.

James, Thurston. *The Prop Builder's Mask-Making Handbook.*
White Hall, Virginia: Betterway Publications, 1990.

Johnstone, Keith. *Impro: Imporvisation and the Theatre.* London:
Methuen, 1990.

Leabhart, Thomas (ed.). "Mime Journal: Number One".
Fayetteville, Arkansas, 1974.

——. "Mime Journal: Number Two". (*Mask Issue.*) Fayetteville,
Arkansas, 1975.

——. "Mime Journal: Numbers Seven and Eight". (*Etienne Decroux
80th Birthday Issue.*) Allendale, Michigan, 1978.

——. "Mime Journal: Numbers Nine and Ten". (*Jacque Copeau's
School for Actors* by Leigh, Barbara Kusler.) Allendale,
Michigan, 1979.

Lecoq, Jacque (ed.). *Le téatre du gest: mimes et acteurs.* Paris:
Bordas, 1987.

Martinez, J.D. *Combat Mime: A Non-Violent Approach to Stage
Violence.* Chicago: Nelson-Hall Publishers, 1982.

Mitter, Shomit. *Systems of Rehearsal: Stanislavsky, Brecht,
Grotowski and Brook.* London: Routledge, 1992.

Pisk, Litz. *The Actor and His Body.* London: Harrap, 1982.

Rea, Kenneth. *A Better Direction*. London: Calouste Gulbenkian Foundation, 1989.

Rolfe, Bari. *Behind the Mask*. Oakland, California: Personabooks, 1977.

—— (ed.) *Mimes on Miming: Writings on the Art of Mime*. London: Millington Books, 1981.

Rood, Arnold (ed.) *Gordon Craig on Movement and Dance*. London: Dance Books, 1978.

Spolin, Viola. *Improvisation for the Theatre*. Evanston, Illinois: Northwestern University Press, 1963.

Stanislavski, Constantine. *An Actor Prepares*. New York: Theatre Arts Books, 1959.

Stanislavski, Constantine. *Building a Character*. London: Methuen, 1992.

Walton, J. Michael (ed.) *Craig on Theatre*. London: Methuen, 1992.

Willett, John (ed.) *Brecht on Theatre*. New York: Hill and Wang, 1964.

Index